"It is better to be a warrior in a garden, than a gardener in a war."

— Miyamoto Musashi, The Book of Five Rings

Although I was never a soldier, while working alongside them for these past 20 years, I have felt myself become eternally connected to the larger family of the men and women who have served and continue to serve the United States Armed Forces. As a child who grew up in foster care without the traditional experience of a typical family, they have brought me into their own and shared the truest sense of the word with me.

Over these many years, I have had the honor of meeting and working with some of the best and brightest, including experiencing the levels of true patriotism and loyalty that are often only spoken of in second-hand accounts from the stories people tell of the times they share.

From the standard sacrifices we take for granted to the ultimate of laying down one's life for our country, it has been a profoundly moving experience for me and my work. From the combat zones to the headquarters, I have been exposed to many perspectives of that larger family. One that I will always support and respect for everything they have given of themselves, the sacrifices their families have made, and the memories we honor along the way.

I dedicate this book to every warrior who is in their own garden ready for war, and to the warriors whose bodies have been laid to rest in the gardens of remembrance.

To the United States Armed Forces, I dedicate this book.

Table of Contents

Dedication 3
Foreward 7
Preface 11

Part One

Introduction 19
Winning Battle Before it Begins 33

Part Two

Choosing Your Battles 53
Be Knowledgeable 61
Be Prepared 71
Be Deceptive 83
Be Formless 93
Be Ready 101
Be Fast 107
Be Victorious 113
Embracing Timeless Wisdom 119

Part Three

The Art of War by Sun Tzu 124
Laying Plans 125
Waging War 128
Attack by Stratagem 131
Tactical Dispositions 134

Table of Contents

Energy	136
Attack by Stratagem	139
Maneuvering	143
Variation in Tactics	146
The Army on the March	148
Terrain	152
The Nine Situations	156
The Attack by Fire	162
The Use of Spies	164
About the Author	170
Also by Jim West	174
Wounded Warrior Project	176

Foreward

In today's digital age, the principles of Sun Tzu's *The Art of War* remain as relevant as ever, especially in the realm of cybersecurity. Jim West's *The Art of War in Cybersecurity* bridges ancient wisdom with contemporary challenges, offering strategic insights that are vital for defending against modern cyberthreats.

Sun Tzu's teachings on leadership, deception, and adaptability—once meant for the battlefield—now provide a guiding framework for cybersecurity professionals. In our interconnected world, where cybersecurity is crucial for protecting national security, corporate integrity, and personal privacy, these principles guide us in safeguarding digital landscapes.

West expertly draws parallels between Sun Tzu's strategies and modern cybersecurity practices. He highlights the importance of thorough planning, the strategic use of deception, and the need for agility in responding to ever-changing threats. Leadership in cybersecurity, as West discusses, goes beyond technical expertise; it requires wisdom, ethical responsibility, and the ability to inspire and lead teams in high-stakes situations.

Moreover, West addresses the ethical dimensions of cybersecurity, echoing Sun Tzu's emphasis on the moral high ground. In a field where decisions impact privacy, trust, and global stability, these ethical considerations are crucial.

The Art of War in Cybersecurity is a call to action for professionals to integrate Sun Tzu's timeless wisdom with the demands of the digital age, ensuring that their strategies are not only effective but also grounded in ethical integrity.

Jaclyn "Jax" Scott
Founder of Outpost Gray

Preface

The irony is not lost on me; to have a successful book, there has to be a lot of preparation before pen meets paper, or in this case, fingers to keyboard. My preparation before creating this book has been working, writing, and speaking on several domains within the field of cybersecurity for more than three decades.

I've taken lessons from every sector I've personally encountered and tried to tie together those lessons with Sun Tzu's lessons to explain how great cybersecurity practices come into existence and survive the test of time. At the heart of my philosophy lie two core beliefs: that planning is everything and that to be effective in any role, you must always be a perpetual student.

In the digital age, where connectivity reigns supreme and information serves as the lifeblood of organizations, the importance of cybersecurity cannot be overstated. With the pervasive nature of cyberthreats, ranging from sophisticated cyber-attacks orchestrated by nation-states to opportunistic exploits by cybercriminals, the critical need for robust cybersecurity measures to safeguard digital assets and preserve organizational resilience only continues to grow.

Every organization, irrespective of size or industry, must meticulously plan and strategize across critical domains, including security, incidents, continuity, and disaster, in order to survive what adversaries may approach us with.

This book endeavors to explore the symbiotic relationship between timeless strategic wisdom, as espoused by the ancient Chinese military philosopher Sun Tzu, and modern cybersecurity principles. Drawing parallels between his teachings and cybersecurity best practices, it aims to elucidate to any individual who picks it up how to fortify defenses, mitigate risks, and emerge victorious in the ever-evolving cyber battlefield.

The Art and War of Cybersecurity is crafted in three main parts. In Part One, I break down the critical overarching themes and concepts I've found in studying Sun Tzu's work to lay a foundation for us to build on. It establishes who history believes Sun Tzu was, more about his work if you are unfamiliar with it, and then what I see are the three key elements of Strategic Thinking.

In Part Two, we move to Sun Tzu's direct teachings,

pairing his quotes and lessons with real-world case studies to see how his principles were either applied effectively or what could have been applied to prevent the particular cybersecurity incident from occurring.

As you read through Part Two, you'll see the parallels continuously overlapping in the real-world case studies. Often, more than one of Sun Tzu's teachings is embodied within them. This truly illustrates what "defense in depth" tries to convey. Leveraging more than one tactic in tandem with others to create multiple layers of security increases the fortitude and resilience of any cybersecurity plan and helps expand any individual's approach to creating and implementing them, too.

Part Three is where I include Lionel Giles' 1910 translation of *The Art of War*. There are at least eight modern translations of the original 13 letters Sun Tzu wrote. Still, it's important to note there are always biases built into any individual who writes the translation and what time in history they're writing from. These invisible influences are very real and shape the final product they produce, much like history itself.

Giles' translation is now part of what's known as the Public Domain. In the United States, his translated work is no longer subject to copyright and can be reprinted and reproduced. I felt it was important to include a copy of *The Art of War* in this work so that you, dear reader, can digest it yourself and find your own insights to take with you moving forward.

As we stand on the precipice of an era with unprecedented technological innovation and digital transformation, the need for a holistic approach, interconnected with the entire scope of cybersecurity, has never been more pressing. By embracing the wisdom of the past and the innovations of the present, we can forge a path toward a secure and resilient future in which organizations thrive amidst the challenges and opportunities of the digital frontier.

Join me on this journey as we embark on a quest to unlock the secrets of cybersecurity excellence. Together, let us chart a course toward a safer, more secure cyber landscape where organizations can flourish in an era of boundless possibility.

Part One

Introduction

A Timeless Guide for Cybersecurity Strategy

Sun Tzu (also known as Sunzi), an ancient Chinese military strategist, philosopher, and author, is best known for his work *The Art of War*. This influential text was composed around 2,500 years ago. Most scholars believe it was written between 475 and 221 B.C.E., during the country's Warring States period. Scholars cannot be sure about the details of the life of the author, but they believe he was a general working for the Wu state. Despite its ambiguous origins, the written work has stood the test of time, continuing to offer profound insights into the nature of conflict, strategy, and leadership. His observations and teachings, though rooted in the context of ancient warfare, transcend the battlefield today, providing valuable lessons applicable to various aspects of contemporary life and several professional practices.

The Art of War is not merely a manual for military commanders; it is a philosophical guide that delves into the complexities of human behavior, decision-making, and the importance of adaptability. Sun Tzu's emphasis on understanding the enemy, leveraging strengths and weaknesses, and the strategic use of deception and surprise reflects a deep comprehension of human psychology and power dynamics. These principles, when applied thoughtfully, can influence business strategies, political maneuvers, and even personal growth, illustrating the universal applicability of Sun Tzu's wisdom.

In today's world, Sun Tzu's teachings find new relevance in cybersecurity. Just as ancient generals had to anticipate and counter the moves of their adversaries, modern cybersecurity professionals must navigate an ever-evolving landscape of threats and vulnerabilities. The strategies outlined in *The Art of War* offer timeless guidance on approaching cybersecurity challenges—emphasizing the importance of intelligence, constant vigilance, and the strategic advantage of maintaining flexibility and resilience in the face of unforeseen attacks.

Moreover, Sun Tzu's work underscores the critical role of preparation and foresight. He advocates for thorough planning, understanding the terrain, and knowing both one's own capabilities and those of the opponent. In cybersecurity, this translates to rigorous threat assessments, robust defenses, and a proactive stance in anticipating potential breaches by adversaries.

Who was Sun Tzu?

Little is known about Sun Tzu's life, and even his exact identity remains a subject of debate among historians. Traditionally, Sun Tzu is believed to have lived during the 6th century BCE, a period marked by considerable political turmoil and frequent warfare in ancient China. According to legend, he served as a military general and strategist under King Helü of Wu. His exact birthplace and early life details are shrouded in mystery, with some accounts suggesting he even hailed from the state of Qi.

Despite the uncertainties surrounding his personal history, Sun Tzu's reputation as a formidable military leader is well-established. He is often depicted as a master strategist whose insights into warfare were far ahead of his time. His role in the military campaigns of King Helü of Wu is particularly noted for demonstrating his strategic prowess and innovative approaches to conflict. These campaigns not only showcased his tactical brilliance but also his ability to understand and manipulate the broader aspects of warfare, including morale, psychology, and logistics.

Sun Tzu's intellectual contributions extended beyond his battlefield exploits. He was also recognized as a philosopher who delved deeply into the nature of conflict, leadership, and human behavior. His philosophical inquiries into the art of strategy and the principles of warfare reflect a keen understanding of both the tangible and intangible elements of conflict. This blend of practical military experience and philosophical inquiry set Sun Tzu apart from his contemporaries, highlighting his unique approach to understanding and addressing the complexities of warfare.

Despite the passage of centuries, the enigmatic figure of Sun Tzu continues to fascinate scholars and military enthusiasts alike. His legacy as a military genius and philosopher endures, even as the details of his life remain elusive. The mystery surrounding his identity only adds to his legendary status, making Sun Tzu a timeless symbol of strategic and philosophical wisdom in the annals of history.

Understanding The Art of War

The Art of War is a timeless masterpiece comprising thirteen chapters, each meticulously focusing on different aspects of military strategy and tactics. Written with precision and insight, each chapter delves into the intricate details of warfare, offering a comprehensive guide that has been revered for centuries. Sun Tzu's work is not just a military manual but a profound treatise on the art of strategy, reflecting his deep understanding of conflict and human nature. The book's structure allows readers to explore various facets of warfare, from the grand strategic level to the tactical nuances of individual engagements.

One of the fundamental themes in *The Art of War* is the importance of planning and preparation. Sun Tzu emphasizes that victory begins long before the first battle is fought. Detailed planning, thorough reconnaissance, and a deep understanding of one's own strengths and weaknesses, as well as those of the enemy, are crucial. This proactive approach to warfare underscores the need for foresight and meticulous preparation, ensuring that every possible scenario is considered and addressed. Sun Tzu's focus on planning highlights his belief that wars are won by the side that is best prepared rather than by sheer force.

Deception plays a pivotal role in Sun Tzu's strategic thinking. He advocates for the use of misdirection and misinformation to confuse and outmaneuver the enemy. A commander can gain significant advantages by creating false impressions and manipulating the opponent's perceptions. Sun Tzu's famous adage, "All warfare is based on deception," encapsulates this principle. The use of deception not only undermines the enemy's confidence but also creates opportunities for decisive actions that can turn the tide of battle. This emphasis on cunning and psychological warfare demonstrates Sun Tzu's recognition of the mind as an equally critical battleground.

Maneuvering and flexibility are also central to Sun Tzu's teachings. He stresses the importance of remaining adaptable and responsive to changing circumstances on the battlefield. A rigid, inflexible approach is doomed to fail, whereas a strategy that can evolve and adapt to the fluid dynamics of conflict will succeed. Sun Tzu uses the analogy of water, which ebbs and flows, adapting to the shape of its container, to illustrate the ideal approach to maneuvering. This concept of strategic flexibility ensures that a commander can exploit opportunities as they arise and respond effectively to unexpected challenges.

Adaptability extends beyond mere maneuvering to encompass the broader strategic mindset advocated by Sun Tzu. He encourages commanders to be creative and innovative, to think outside the conventional norms of warfare. This forward-thinking approach enables leaders to devise unique solutions tailored to their specific conditions and challenges. His teachings promote a dynamic and evolving strategy, one that leverages surprise and innovation to maintain the advantage and keep the enemy off balance. This adaptability is not just a tactical necessity but a fundamental aspect of strategic superiority.

Finally, central to Sun Tzu's philosophy is the idea of achieving victory through strategic superiority rather than relying solely on brute force. He argues that the most successful commanders are those who can win without fighting and who can achieve their objectives through strategic maneuvering, diplomacy, and the intelligent application of force. This approach minimizes unnecessary loss and destruction, achieving goals efficiently and precisely. His concept of strategic superiority emphasizes the importance of intelligence, planning, and psychological insight, making *The Art of War* a timeless guide not just for military leaders but for anyone seeking to navigate complex challenges and conflicts with wisdom and skill.

Historical and Present-Day Influence

Throughout history, *The Art of War* has been studied and applied by military leaders, politicians, business executives, and scholars worldwide. Its principles have profoundly shaped historical figures such as Napoleon Bonaparte, Mao Zedong, and General Douglas MacArthur, who all drew from Sun Tzu's insights to craft their own strategic doctrines. The universality of Sun Tzu's teachings lies in their ability to transcend the specifics of ancient Chinese warfare and offer timeless guidance applicable to various forms of conflict and competition.

Military leaders, in particular, have found *The Art of War* to be an invaluable resource. The emphasis on thorough preparation, the strategic use of deception, and the importance of flexibility have resonated deeply with commanders across different eras and cultures. For instance, during World War II, Allied and Axis powers studied Sun Tzu's strategies to outmaneuver their opponents. The Cold War era also saw military theorists and strategists incorporating Sun Tzu's principles into their global power dynamics and nuclear deterrence analyses.

Beyond the battlefield, Sun Tzu's teachings have found a significant place in the realms of politics and diplomacy. Politicians and diplomats have utilized his concepts of strategic thinking, psychological warfare, and the art of negotiation to gain advantages in both domestic and international arenas. The emphasis on understanding the opponent, anticipating their moves, and strategically positioning oneself has been instrumental in achieving diplomatic victories and forging alliances. Sun Tzu's influence is evident in crafting policies and strategies prioritizing long-term gains and stability over short-term triumphs.

In the business world, *The Art of War* has become a cornerstone for executives and entrepreneurs seeking to navigate competitive markets. The principles of strategic planning, resource management, and the importance of adaptability are as relevant in boardrooms as they are on battlefields. Business leaders often draw parallels between market competition and military conflict, applying Sun Tzu's tactics to gain a competitive edge, manage risks, and achieve organizational goals. Concepts such as "knowing the enemy," "winning without fighting," and leveraging one's strengths against competitors' weaknesses have become integral to strategic business planning and operations.

The world of sports, too, has embraced Sun Tzu's wisdom. Coaches and athletes apply his teachings to develop strategies, build mental resilience, and outmaneuver their opponents. The focus on preparation, adaptability, and the psychological aspects of competition aligns closely with the demands of high-performance sports. Sun Tzu's emphasis on understanding both oneself and the adversary has helped teams and individuals achieve success by fostering a deeper strategic mindset and a disciplined approach to training and competition.

In conclusion, *The Art of War* continues to be a vital source of strategic wisdom across various domains. Its principles have shaped historical and contemporary approaches to conflict, competition, and leadership. From military leaders to business executives, politicians to athletes, Sun Tzu's teachings remain relevant and influential, offering timeless guidance for navigating the complexities of human endeavor. The enduring legacy's strength lies in its ability to provide strategic clarity and insight, making it an essential read for anyone seeking to master the art of strategy in their respective fields.

Relevance to Cybersecurity

In our modern era, the principles outlined in *The Art of War* are remarkably relevant to the field of cybersecurity. In an increasingly complex and dynamic cyber landscape, organizations face adversaries who employ tactics akin to those described by Sun Tzu. By applying his teachings, cybersecurity professionals can gain valuable insights into threat intelligence, risk management, incident response, and strategic planning.

As cyberthreats become increasingly sophisticated, the strategic principles outlined in *The Art of War* provide valuable guidance for defending against attacks. The emphasis on intelligence, deception, and adaptability is particularly relevant in cybersecurity, where understanding the tactics of cyber adversaries and staying ahead of potential threats is crucial. Cybersecurity professionals apply Sun Tzu's teachings to develop proactive defense strategies, conduct threat assessments, and respond swiftly and effectively to breaches. The art of cyber warfare, much like traditional warfare, benefits from Sun Tzu's timeless insights into strategy and human behavior.

In the realm of threat intelligence, Sun Tzu's emphasis on knowing the enemy is paramount. Just as military leaders must understand their opponents' strategies, strengths, and weaknesses, cybersecurity experts must gather and analyze data about potential threats and attackers. This involves monitoring cyber activities, studying the techniques and patterns used by cybercriminals, their organizations, and predicting future attacks based on current trends. Sun Tzu's principle of deception is equally applicable, as cybersecurity professionals can use misinformation and honeypots to mislead and trap attackers, thereby gaining critical information about their methods and objectives.

Risk management in cybersecurity can also benefit from Sun Tzu's strategic insights. His advocacy for thorough planning and preparation resonates with the need for robust cybersecurity frameworks and policies. Organizations must identify their most valuable assets, assess vulnerabilities, and implement measures to protect against potential threats. Sun Tzu's focus on flexibility and adaptability is crucial as the cyber threat landscape continually evolves. By staying agile and ready to adapt to new threats, cybersecurity teams can ensure that their defenses remain effective against emerging risks.

Incident response is another area in which Sun Tzu's teachings are highly relevant. His counsel on maintaining calm and decisiveness in the face of conflict applies directly to managing cyber incidents. When a breach occurs, the ability to quickly assess the situation, contain the threat, and mitigate damage is vital. Sun Tzu's advice on using strategic surprise and swift, decisive action can guide incident response teams in neutralizing threats before they can cause significant harm. Furthermore, his principle of leveraging one's strengths to exploit the enemy's weaknesses can inform the development of tailored response strategies that turn the tide in favor of the defenders.

Strategic planning in cybersecurity, much like in warfare, requires a comprehensive understanding of the internal environment and the external threat landscape. Sun Tzu's holistic approach to strategy—considering factors such as terrain, morale, and leadership—can be adapted to the digital realm. Cybersecurity leaders must evaluate their organization's infrastructure, culture, and capabilities while also staying informed about the broader cybersecurity ecosystem. By integrating Sun Tzu's strategic principles into their planning processes, organizations can create resilient, proactive cybersecurity strategies that effectively anticipate and counteract potential threats.

How Cybersecurity Can Benefit

Cybersecurity practitioners can draw upon Sun Tzu's wisdom to develop more effective defense strategies, anticipate adversaries' moves, and respond decisively to cyberthreats. The modern cyber landscape is a battleground where attackers and defenders continuously engage in a high-stakes game of strategy and tactics. By integrating Sun Tzu's principles, cybersecurity professionals can enhance their approach to protecting digital assets and maintaining the integrity of their systems.

One core tenet of Sun Tzu's philosophy is using deception to mislead and confuse the enemy. In cybersecurity, this translates to employing tactics such as honeypots, decoy networks, and false information to divert attackers from actual targets. By creating an environment of uncertainty and unpredictability, defenders can cause attackers to waste resources and time, ultimately reducing the likelihood of a successful breach. Deception techniques, inspired by Sun Tzu, can serve as powerful tools in a cybersecurity professional's arsenal, making it significantly harder for adversaries to achieve their objectives.

Maneuvering is another key concept in *The Art of War* that is equally applicable to cybersecurity. Just as Sun Tzu advocated for the strategic movement of troops to gain a positional advantage, cybersecurity practitioners must be agile in their approach. This involves constantly updating and rotating security measures, employing dynamic defense mechanisms, and staying ahead of emerging threats. By maneuvering deftly within the digital landscape, organizations can maintain a defensive posture that is both proactive and reactive, ready to counteract any attempts by adversaries to exploit vulnerabilities.

Adaptability is crucial in the ever-evolving world of cybersecurity. Sun Tzu's teachings emphasize the importance of being flexible and responsive to changing circumstances. Cybersecurity professionals must adopt a mindset of continuous improvement, regularly reassessing and updating their security protocols to address new and evolving threats. This requires staying informed about the latest developments in cyber-attack techniques, investing in ongoing education and training, and fostering a culture of vigilance and readiness. By embodying Sun Tzu's principle of adaptability, organizations can ensure that their defenses remain robust and resilient in the face of an ever-changing threat landscape.

Sun Tzu's emphasis on strategic superiority and proactive preparation resonates profoundly in the context of cybersecurity. He advocated for thorough preparation and planning, which is essential for building a strong cybersecurity posture. This involves conducting regular risk assessments, developing comprehensive incident response plans, and ensuring that all stakeholders are aware of and trained in their roles. By anticipating potential threats and preparing accordingly, organizations can minimize the impact of cyber-attacks and respond more effectively when incidents occur.

Proactive preparation also means investing in advanced threat detection and response technologies, implementing multi-layered security defenses, and fostering a culture of security awareness throughout the organization. Just as Sun Tzu's victorious generals won battles without fighting, the most effective cybersecurity strategies prevent incidents before they can happen through careful planning and proactive measures.

By embracing Sun Tzu's concepts, such as deception, maneuvering, adaptability, and proactive preparation, organizations can significantly strengthen their cyber defenses and mitigate risks more effectively. Sun Tzu's wisdom on strategic superiority provides a timeless framework for navigating the complexities of modern cybersecurity, where the ability to outmaneuver adversaries and anticipate their moves is paramount to success.

As cyberthreats continue to evolve, the principles outlined in *The Art of War* remain as relevant and applicable as ever, guiding cybersecurity professionals in their quest to protect and defend critical digital assets.

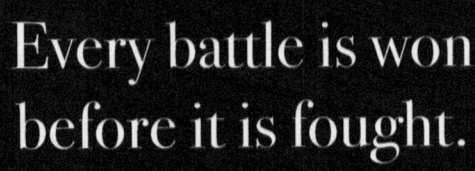

> "Every battle is won before it is fought."
> — Sun Tzu, *The Art of War*

> "Planning is everything. Every organization should have plans for security, incidents, continuity, disaster, etc."
> — Jim West, Cybersecurity Expert

The Beginning

Winning the Cybersecurity Battle Before it Begins

Today, battles are fought on land, sea, air, space, and now, in this ever-expanding digital world online. While time has changed the tools and adversaries, drawing parallels between ancient military strategy and modern cybersecurity practices, *The Art of War* continues to illuminate the path to effective and strategic problem-solving, proving its enduring relevance and value.

In the realm of cybersecurity, where the battleground is virtual and the adversaries are often faceless, the wisdom of Sun Tzu finds profound resonance. Among his timeless teachings, one particular axiom stands out, "Every battle is won before it is fought." In the context of cybersecurity, this adage holds immense significance, heralding the importance of preparation, foresight, and innovation in securing digital assets against ever-evolving threats.

Lofty Ideals

The overarching universal goal of cybersecurity is to ensure the secure storage, controlled access, and prevention of the unauthorized processing, transfer, or deletion of data. Like warfare, cybersecurity demands meticulous planning and proactive measures to ensure victory.

When these broad concepts are often discussed, they can feel like an effervescent and lofty ideal everyone wants to reach, but no clear objectives have been given. The inverse challenge can be true as well, where you have concrete goals needing to be met, but no rationale or proper context is given as to why it's so important they be met.

By now, you have likely attended monthly, quarterly, or annual strategic planning meetings where leadership speaks about their vision, goals, and the directions they would like for the team, department, or organization to head in. They focus on why this approach matters, but then the momentum is lost when determining how they plan to reach these goals.

The same applies to "strategic thinking," where leaders want to see their teams capable of high performance but often fail to achieve this objective.

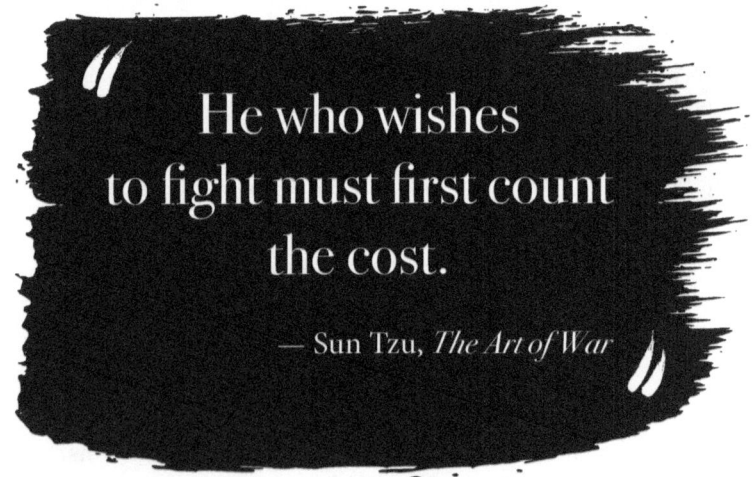

> He who wishes to fight must first count the cost.
>
> — Sun Tzu, *The Art of War*

The Three Keys of Strategic Thinking

It is no surprise that a military general at Sun Tzu's level was concerned with strategy and the execution of meticulously laid plans. Strategy, after all, is how you achieve one or more long-term or overall goals under conditions of uncertainty. But what does it mean to think strategically?

Strategic thinking in cybersecurity can be boiled down to three key concepts: preparation, foresight, and innovation. In short, strategic thinking is the implementation of the long-term goal of moving beyond reactive measures, such as putting out daily fires, and toward proactive strategies that address current and future threats.

Foresight

All foresight is based on judgment.

We first focus on judgment and foresight because these two elements directly influence and change our strategy, plans, and actions. You can't prepare for a plan that doesn't exist, and you can't find new ways of doing things if you don't know the long-term and short-term goals when searching for new solutions.

In decision-making and critical thinking, judgment plays a crucial role in evaluating options and choosing the best course of action. In short, it helps you count the cost of the decision before and after it's made. Different types of judgment can be categorized based on how decisions are made, the context in which they are made, and the level of reasoning involved.

The Eight (main) Types of Judgment

1. Intuitive Judgment
This involves making decisions based on gut feelings or instinct. Intuitive judgment is often quick and based on experience or inherent understanding rather than deliberate analysis.
> **Example:** A firefighter decides the best way to exit a burning building based on instinct developed through years of experience.
> **Strengths:** Fast and efficient in situations where time is critical.
> **Limitations:** It may be biased or inaccurate, especially in unfamiliar situations.

2. Analytical Judgment
This involves a systematic and logical approach to decision-making. It requires breaking down a problem into smaller parts, evaluating each part, and synthesizing the information to make a decision.
> **Example:** A business analyst assesses market trends, financial reports, and consumer behavior before recommending a strategic move.
> **Strengths:** Thorough and minimizes the risk of errors.
> **Limitations:** Time-consuming and may be less effective in urgent situations.

3. Heuristic Judgment
This relies on mental shortcuts or rules of thumb to make decisions. Heuristics simplify the decision-making process by focusing on critical aspects of the problem, often at the expense of thoroughness.
> **Example:** Choosing a product based on brand reputation rather than comparing all available options.
> **Strengths:** Efficient and works well for routine decisions.

Limitations: This can lead to cognitive biases and errors.

4. Moral Judgment

This involves decisions based on ethical principles or moral considerations. This type of judgment weighs the rightness or wrongness of actions based on values and societal norms.

Example: Deciding to whistleblow on corporate malpractice despite potential personal consequences.
Strengths: Upholds ethical standards and societal values.
Limitations: Can be subjective and conflict with practical considerations.

5. Legal Judgment

Laws, regulations, and legal precedents guide this type of decision-making. Legal judgment requires interpreting and applying legal principles to specific situations.

Example: A judge ruling on a case by applying existing laws and considering previous similar cases.
Strengths: Provides consistency and predictability in decision-making.
Limitations: This may be rigid and not account for unique circumstances.

6. Reflective Judgment

This involves careful consideration and self-reflection before making a decision. Reflective judgment is characterized by evaluating evidence, considering multiple perspectives, and acknowledging the complexity of the issue.

Example: A leader considering the long-term implications of a policy change, reflecting on past experiences, and consulting various stakeholders.
Strengths: Leads to well-rounded and informed decisions.
Limitations: Time-intensive and may lead to indecision if overdone.

7. Pragmatic Judgment
This focuses on practical outcomes and the feasibility of decisions. The pragmatic judgment considers a decision's immediate and realistic impacts rather than ideal or theoretical outcomes.
> **Example:** A project manager deciding to delay a product launch to ensure quality, balancing potential market risks with the practicalities of production.
> **Strengths:** Realistic and grounded in practicality.
> **Limitations:** May overlook long-term or broader considerations.

8. Creative Judgment
This involves innovative thinking and the exploration of unconventional solutions. Creative judgment pushes the boundaries of traditional decision-making by considering novel ideas and approaches.
> **Example:** An advertising agency developing a unique campaign strategy that deviates from industry norms.
> **Strengths:** Encourages innovation and differentiation.
> **Limitations:** Can be risky and untested.

Each type of judgment has its place in decision-making and critical thinking. Influential decision-makers often use a combination of these judgments depending on the context, the nature of the decision, and the desired outcomes. Balancing these different approaches can lead to more robust and effective decisions. The key, once again, is remaining flexible.

Planning and Preparation

To be frank, planning and preparation sound the least exciting of the three key principles of Strategic Thinking, but do not let impatience and short-sightedness be the downfall of this trifecta.

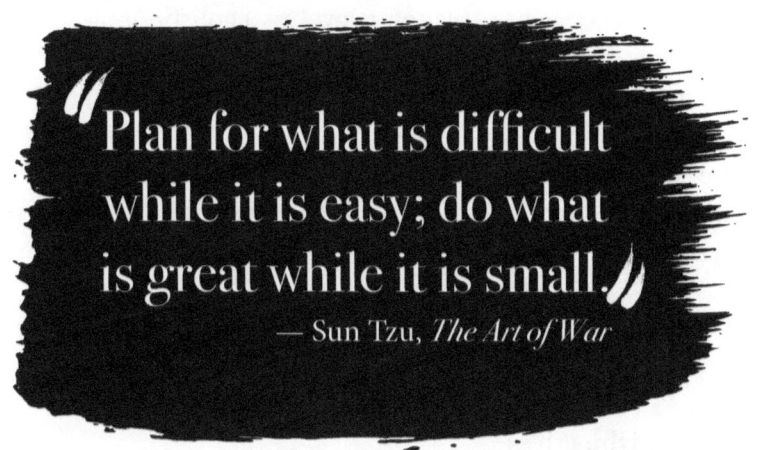

> "Plan for what is difficult while it is easy; do what is great while it is small."
> — Sun Tzu, *The Art of War*

A plan does not have to be perfect to work, but it does need to be flexible enough to adapt to changing circumstances so that when things change, you swiftly regroup and continue moving forward.

In more contemporary terms, we've heard the adage, "An ounce of prevention is worth a pound of cure." This is nothing new. In cybersecurity, our prevention methods are usually broken down into the following: Risk Assessment, Security Policies and Procedures, Architecture and Controls, Identity and Access Management, Training and Awareness, Incident Response and Recovery, Continuous Monitoring and Improvement, and finally, Compliance and Legal considerations.

The crux of any team, department, or organization is building continuous improvement into our preparations and planning so that feedback is captured and implemented quickly rather than stored for later or, worse, ignored altogether. Organizations must remain vigilant and adaptive, regularly updating their cybersecurity plans to address emerging threats and changes in any environment.

Effective cybersecurity planning involves a holistic approach that integrates risk management, technical controls, policies, and continuous improvement. But what makes an effective plan?

The core principles of good planning and preparation are fundamental to success in any endeavor. Here's a breakdown of each:

The Nine Parts of a Plan

1. Clear Objectives
Define specific, measurable, achievable, relevant, and time-bound (SMART) goals. Knowing precisely what you aim to achieve is the foundation of good planning.

2. Comprehensive Research
Gather all relevant information and data. Understanding the context, resources, risks, and opportunities is crucial to formulating an effective plan.

3. Prioritization
Identify and focus on the most critical tasks and objectives. This helps in allocating resources and time effectively.

4. Flexibility and Adaptability
Plans should be adaptable to changes. Being able to pivot or adjust the plan as circumstances change is essential for long-term success.

5. Resource Allocation
Determine the resources (time, money, personnel, etc.) needed and allocate them appropriately. Ensure that there is a balance between needs and available resources.

6. Timeline and Milestones
Establish a clear timeline with milestones to track progress. This helps in maintaining momentum and ensures that the plan stays on course.

7. Risk Management
Identify potential risks and develop contingency plans. This involves anticipating challenges and having strategies in place to mitigate them.

8. Collaboration and Communication
Ensure that all stakeholders are involved in the planning process and that there is clear communication throughout. Collaboration helps in gaining different perspectives and buy-in.

9. Evaluation and Feedback
Regularly assess the plan's progress and effectiveness. Be open to feedback and make necessary adjustments to improve the plan.

Core Principles of Good Preparation

Good preparation is the cornerstone of success in any endeavor, whether a significant project, a critical event, or daily tasks. Preparation goes beyond simply getting ready; it involves a systematic approach that ensures you are fully equipped to face whatever lies ahead. The principles of good preparation are designed to help you anticipate challenges, organize your resources, and optimize your performance. By adhering to these principles, you can confidently approach any situation, knowing that you've done everything possible to ensure a successful outcome.

Let's explore the nine core principles of good preparation that will guide you toward excellence and readiness in all your pursuits.

The Nine Parts of Preparation

1. Detailed Understanding
A thorough understanding of what is required, including the objectives, expectations, and potential challenges.

2. Organization
Organize all necessary tools, resources, and information in advance. This includes preparing materials, setting up systems, and ensuring everything is in place before starting.

3. Skill Development
Ensure that the necessary skills are developed or refreshed. This could involve training, practice, or research to ensure readiness.

4. Mental and Physical Readiness
Preparation also involves being mentally and physically ready for the task. This could include rest, nutrition, mindset, and stress management.

5. Contingency Planning
Prepare for unexpected situations by having backup plans. This means thinking ahead about what could go wrong and being ready to address it.

6. Attention to Detail
Pay close attention to the finer details. Success in preparation often involves addressing the small but crucial aspects of the task at hand.

7. Time Management
Allocate sufficient time for preparation. Avoid last-minute rushes by starting early and allowing time for revisions and adjustments.

8. Testing and Rehearsal
If applicable, test or rehearse the plan or task. This can help identify potential issues and improve performance.

9. Documentation
Keep records or notes of the preparation process. This can be useful for future reference or for making adjustments as needed.

Both good planning and preparation are iterative processes that benefit from continuous improvement and reflection. By adhering to these principles, you can significantly increase the likelihood of achieving your goals efficiently and effectively.

Innovation

Finally, we reach innovation. This is usually where individuals are the most excited to apply their time and resources because we're human and love the feeling of accomplishment when we can find creative solutions.

Innovation is often described as a process, not surprisingly, as one that involves a series of steps or stages leading from the germination of an idea to its full realization as a novel and impactful solution. This process is dynamic and iterative, often involving cycles of refinement and adaptation rather than a linear progression. At its core, innovation requires the intersection of creativity, knowledge, and practical application.

The process begins with problem identification or opportunity recognition. This is the stage where a need is identified—whether it's a gap in the market, an inefficiency in a system, or a social issue needing resolution. In academic and research contexts, this may stem from a gap in existing literature or a new question arising from previous findings. The innovator, or the team, must deeply understand the context, involving comprehensive research and data collection to frame the problem accurately.

Once the problem is well-defined, the next stage is idea generation. This phase leverages creativity, brainstorming, and divergent thinking to generate a wide array of possible solutions. At this stage, it's essential to encourage wild ideas and diverse perspectives, as innovation often thrives on the unconventional.

Following idea generation, the process moves into evaluation and selection. Here, the innovator assesses the feasibility, scalability, and potential impact of each idea. This stage involves critical thinking and may require preliminary tests, simulations, or pilot studies to gauge viability. In educational settings, this may also affect peer review or feedback from experts in the field.

Once a promising idea is identified, the next phase is development and prototyping. This is where the idea takes a tangible form. It could involve designing a model, creating a prototype, or drafting a detailed plan. The aim is to bring the concept into a more concrete phase where its practical application can be assessed. This stage is iterative, often requiring multiple prototyping, testing, and refinement rounds.

Implementation follows development. This stage moves the innovation from concept to reality. It involves the actual creation or execution of the idea, whether launching a new product, introducing a new teaching method, or applying a new theory in practice. This stage often requires navigating logistical challenges, scaling the solution, and addressing unforeseen issues that arise during implementation.

Finally, the process culminates in evaluation and diffusion. Once implemented, the innovation is assessed for its effectiveness, impact, and sustainability. This involves collecting data, analyzing outcomes, and making adjustments as needed. If successful, the innovation may then be diffused or spread more broadly, whether through publication, commercialization, or adoption by other institutions or organizations.

Throughout this process, it's essential to recognize the role of feedback loops. Innovation is rarely a straight path; instead, it often requires revisiting earlier stages based on new insights or challenges encountered along the way. This iterative nature allows for continuous improvement and adaptation, making innovation not just a process but a journey of discovery and refinement.

Do Not Operate in a Vacuum

Moreover, innovation doesn't occur in a vacuum. It often involves collaboration, drawing on the expertise and creativity of a diverse group of people. In academic settings, this might mean interdisciplinary work, where different fields come together to tackle complex problems from multiple angles. In practice, it could involve partnerships between academia, industry, and the public sector.

Conclusion

In conclusion, innovation is a complex, dynamic, and

iterative journey that moves from problem identification to idea generation, through development and implementation, and finally to evaluation and diffusion. It requires a balance of creativity and critical thinking and the ability to navigate uncertainty and complexity. For those engaged in this process, it offers the opportunity to not only solve problems but to push the boundaries of what is possible, creating new value and making a lasting impact.

You'll notice that all three elements of Strategic Thinking highlight an iterative process, meaning there's a continual push toward improvement using feedback. If feedback in a team, department, or organization isn't a two-way road, then operations, efficiency, and efficacy will deteriorate over time.

In the digital age, where cyberthreats loom large and the stakes are higher than ever, Sun Tzu's timeless wisdom is a guiding light for cybersecurity practitioners worldwide. By embracing the philosophy that "every battle is won before it is fought," organizations can proactively fortify their defenses, anticipate adversaries' moves, and emerge victorious in the ever-evolving cyber battlefield. Through strategic planning, resource allocation, deception, and a steadfast commitment to vigilance, organizations can turn the tide in their favor, ensuring the security and integrity of their digital assets in an increasingly hostile digital landscape.

"The general who wins a battle makes many calculations in his temple ere the battle is fought. The general who loses a battle makes but few calculations beforehand. Thus do many calculations lead to victory, and few calculations to defeat: how much more no calculation at all! It is by attention to this point that I can foresee who is likely to win or lose."

— Sun Tzu, *The Art of War*

> To be an effective leader, you have to weigh each decision with its actual cost. If you try to fight every battle, then there will be nothing left for the ones that truly matter.
>
> — Jim West, Cybersecurity Expert

Chapter 1

Choosing Your Battles

The Eight Applied Principles of Sun Tzu

We begin our journey into Sun Tzu's teachings with one of his most poignant reminders, "He who exercises no forethought but makes light of his opponents is sure to be captured by them." With any conflict, weighing the decisions before they are made is essential to creating a favorable outcome.

Achieving Security Without Conflict

Sun Tzu's maxim, "The supreme art of war is to subdue the enemy without fighting," embodies the pinnacle of strategic mastery. In cybersecurity, this principle translates to preventing attacks and neutralizing threats without direct confrontation, relying instead on deterrence, resilience, and the strategic use of technology and intelligence. This chapter delves into how Sun Tzu's philosophy of non-confrontational victory informs modern cybersecurity strategies, illustrating this through examples where silent but potent measures have safeguarded the digital domain.

Strategic Deployment of Resources

Sun Tzu emphasizes the judicious allocation of resources to

maximize their effectiveness on the battlefield. Similarly, in cybersecurity, organizations must strategically deploy their resources - be it personnel, technology, or budgetary allocations - to address the most pressing security concerns and mitigate risks effectively.

Prioritizing vulnerabilities based on their severity and potential impact on business operations enables organizations to allocate resources where they are most needed. Additionally, investing in advanced cybersecurity solutions, such as intrusion detection systems, endpoint protection platforms, and threat intelligence tools, empowers organizations to proactively identify and neutralize threats before they escalate into full-blown cyber incidents.

Case Studies

The Power of Deterrence: The FBI's Operation Bot Roast

A compelling illustration of cyber deterrence in action is the FBI's Operation Bot Roast. Initiated in 2007, this operation targeted botnet operations, resulting in the identification and disruption of several large-scale botnets responsible for a variety of cybercrimes. By publicizing the arrests of botnet operators and the dismantling of their networks, the operation served as a potent deterrent, signaling to potential cybercriminals the high risks associated with such activities. The operation showcased how law enforcement agencies could subdue cyberthreats without direct engagement by making the consequences of such actions clear and significant (FBI, 2007).

Enhancing Resilience: Estonia's Cyber Resilience Post-2007

Following a devastating series of cyber-attacks in 2007, Estonia embarked on an extensive program to bolster its national cyber resilience. This included the establishment of the NATO Cooperative Cyber Defense Centre of Excellence in Tallinn, extensive public-private partnerships in cyber defense, and widespread public education on cyber hygiene. Through these efforts, Estonia enhanced its digital infrastructure's resilience, making it one of the most cyber-secure nations in the world. Estonia's strategy effectively subdues potential attackers by demonstrating that the nation can quickly recover from attacks, thus diminishing the attackers' motivations (NATO CCD COE, 2008).

Strategic Use of Technology and Intelligence: The Deployment of AI in Cyber Defense

An example of subduing the enemy without fighting through technology is the use of artificial intelligence (AI) in cybersecurity. AI algorithms can analyze vast amounts of data to detect patterns indicative of a cyber threat, often identifying and mitigating these threats before they can manifest into attacks. For instance, in 2016, DARPA hosted the Cyber Grand Challenge, a competition aimed at advancing AI capabilities in cyber defense. The winning team's AI system demonstrated an ability to autonomously identify and patch vulnerabilities in real-time, showcasing the potential of AI to subdue cyberthreats silently and efficiently (DARPA, 2016).

Conclusion

Sun Tzu's principle of achieving victory without conflict finds profound application in cybersecurity. Through strategies that emphasize deterrence, resilience, and the strategic use of technology and intelligence, cybersecurity professionals can effectively subdue potential threats without direct engagement. The examples of Operation Bot Roast, Estonia's cyber resilience efforts, and the advent of AI in cyber defense illustrate how these non-confrontational approaches align with Sun Tzu's teachings, offering a path to security and stability in the digital age.

What's more, Sun Tzu also focuses on not fighting needlessly, saying that it is better to escape and regroup than to die needlessly. Resources are finite, and there is a limit to how far you can push the envelope before things collapse.

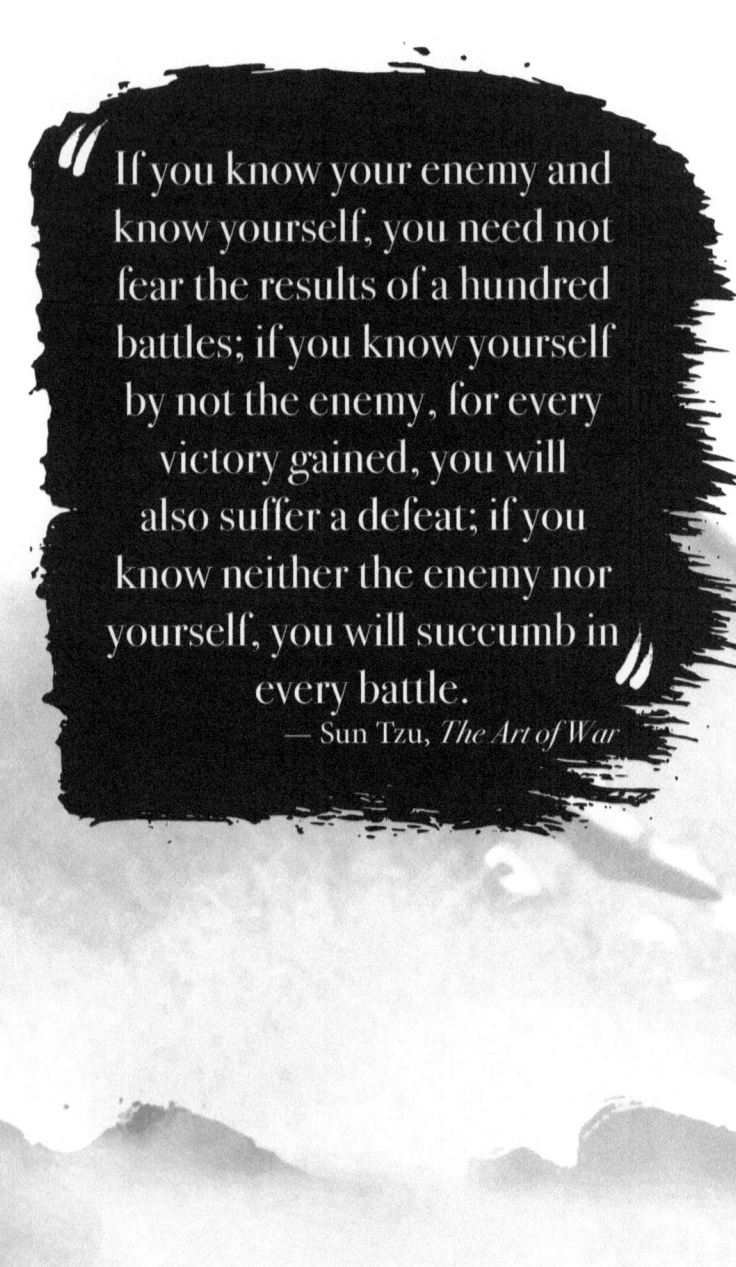

> If you know your enemy and know yourself, you need not fear the results of a hundred battles; if you know yourself by not the enemy, for every victory gained, you will also suffer a defeat; if you know neither the enemy nor yourself, you will succumb in every battle.
> — Sun Tzu, *The Art of War*

> Today's cybersecurity expert must not only continuously monitor their organiza-tion for risks but also continuously monitor the news, threat intelligence feeds, and continue to learn about new technologies. As attacks evolve, so must the focus of the continuous monitoring.
>
> — Jim West, Cybersecurity Expert

Chapter 2

Be Knowledgeable

The Foundations of Cyber Resilience

In *The Art of War*, the maxim "Know Thyself" serves as a cornerstone of strategic wisdom. In cybersecurity, this principle holds profound significance, emphasizing the critical importance of self-awareness, introspection, and understanding one's strengths and weaknesses in the face of ever-evolving cyberthreats.

Understanding Your Digital Terrain

Before embarking on any strategic endeavor, it is essential to gain a comprehensive understanding of your digital terrain - the interconnected web of networks, systems, applications, and data repositories that constitute your organization's IT infrastructure. This requires a thorough assessment of your assets, vulnerabilities, and risk exposure, enabling you to identify potential points of weakness and fortify your defenses accordingly.

Conducting Cyber Hygiene Assessments

Conducting Cyber Hygiene Assessments is a fundamental

practice that supports an organization's ability to be deeply knowledgeable about its cyber terrain, which is critical in maintaining a strong cybersecurity posture, thus thoroughly "knowing yourself" to address strengths and weaknesses.

Any organization's digital terrain includes its networks, systems, applications, data repositories, and the interconnections between them. Being knowledgeable about this terrain means understanding every aspect of the organization's digital footprint—where potential vulnerabilities lie, how data flows through the system, and where critical assets are located.

Cyber Hygiene Assessments are systematic evaluations of an organization's cybersecurity practices, focusing on the effectiveness and thoroughness of security controls and protocols. These assessments involve a detailed examination of the organization's infrastructure, including hardware, software, and user practices, to identify vulnerabilities, assess risks, and ensure compliance with cybersecurity standards and best practices.

By conducting regular Cyber Hygiene Assessments, an organization gains a comprehensive and up-to-date understanding of its cyber terrain by:

     1. Mapping the Digital Landscape
     2. Identifying Vulnerabilities and Gaps
     3. Understanding Data Flows and Access Points
     4. Assessing User Practices and Behavior
     5. Ensuring Compliance and Best Practices
     6. Facilitating Continuous Improvement

Cyber Hygiene Assessments are not one-time events but part of an ongoing process of continuous improvement. Each assessment provides new insights into the cyber terrain, highlighting areas for improvement and documenting progress over time. This iterative process ensures that the organization's knowledge of its cyber terrain evolves alongside the changing threat landscape.

By continuously refining and enhancing cybersecurity practices, the organization stays ahead of potential threats and maintains a robust defense posture.

In summary, conducting Cyber Hygiene Assessments is essential for maintaining a deep and current understanding of an organization's "self." These assessments map the digital landscape, identify vulnerabilities, analyze data flows, assess user behavior, ensure compliance, and support continuous improvement. By doing so, they provide the knowledge needed to protect critical assets, mitigate risks, and respond effectively to emerging threats.

Harnessing the Power of Threat Intelligence

In Sun Tzu's teachings, knowledge of the enemy's intentions and capabilities is paramount to achieving victory. In cybersecurity, threat intelligence serves as the modern-day equivalent, providing organizations with valuable insights into the tactics, techniques, and procedures employed by cyber adversaries. By leveraging threat intelligence feeds, organizations can proactively identify and mitigate emerging threats, enhancing their cyber resilience.

Understanding the Adversary's Tactics and Intentions

Just as Sun Tzu emphasizes the importance of knowing one's enemy, cybersecurity practitioners must strive to understand the tactics, techniques, and motivations of cyber adversaries. Organizations can gain valuable insights into their adversaries' methods and intentions by analyzing past attacks, studying threat intelligence reports, and monitoring the dark web for chatter and indicators of compromise.

Exploiting Weaknesses and Creating Opportunities

Sun Tzu's teachings underscore the importance of exploiting adversaries' weaknesses and capitalizing on opportunities for victory. This translates to identifying and exploiting vulnerabilities in adversaries' infrastructure, tactics, and techniques in cybersecurity. Organizations can pinpoint weaknesses in adversaries' defenses by conducting thorough vulnerability assessments, penetration tests, and adversary emulation exercises and mount effective countermeasures.

Case Studies

Knowing Yourself: The Heartbleed Vulnerability

In 2014, the Heartbleed bug revealed a critical vulnerability in the OpenSSL cryp-tographic software library, which could allow attackers to read sensitive data from the memory of millions of web servers. OpenSSL was widely used for securing websites, making the potential impact vast. The organizations that quickly identified their exposure to Heartbleed were those with a strong understanding of their own digital envi-ronments. These entities had detailed inventories of their systems and knew exactly where OpenSSL was deployed, facilitating rapid patching and mitigation efforts. This incident underscores the importance of self-knowledge in manag-ing cybersecurity risks (British Broadcasting Corporation, 2014).

Knowing the Enemy: The WannaCry Ransomware Attack

In May 2017, the WannaCry ransomware attack affected over 230,000 computers in over 150 countries, exploiting vulnerabilities in outdated Windows operating systems. The attack highlighted the importance of understanding cyberthreats, as the exploited vulnerability had been patched by Microsoft two months prior to the attack. However, many organizations had not applied the update, primarily due to a lack of awareness of the threat it mitigated. In contrast, organizations that had prioritized threat intelligence were either unaffected or able to respond quickly, demonstrating the significance of knowing the enemy in cybersecurity (National Cyber Security Centre, 2017).

Knowing the Enemy: The Targeted Defense Against SolarWinds

The SolarWinds hack, a sophisticated cyber espionage operation discovered in December 2020, compromised thousands of organizations worldwide. However, certain entities were able to avoid damage by leveraging advanced threat intelligence. Microsoft, for instance, quickly identified the malicious code hidden within the SolarWinds Orion platform update and took swift action to mitigate the threat. By understanding the tactics used by the nation-state actors behind the attack, Microsoft was able to isolate affected systems and prevent further damage (Microsoft Security Response Center, 2020). This example epitomizes the value of knowing one's enemy in the cybersecurity domain, demonstrating how deep insights into adversarial tactics can enable effective preemptive defenses.

The Interplay of Knowing Yourself and Your Enemy: The NotPetya Malware Incident

In June 2017, the NotPetya malware wreaked havoc worldwide, initially targeting organizations in Ukraine before spreading globally. NotPetya masqueraded as ransomware but was primarily designed to disrupt and destroy. The companies that navigated the NotPetya incident most successfully were those that not only understood their own IT infrastructures but also actively engaged with threat intelligence services to anticipate such attacks. One such company, a global shipping giant, was able to mitigate the impact by quickly isolating infected systems and leveraging backups to restore operations. This response was possible due to a strong grasp of both their digital environment and the nature of the threat, illustrating the critical balance of self-knowledge and enemy insight in cybersecurity (Wired, 2018).

Understanding the Battlefield: The JPMorgan Chase Breach "Prevention"

In 2014, JPMorgan Chase, one of the largest banks in the United States, was targeted by hackers in what could have been a catastrophic data breach. However, unlike other victims, JPMorgan had invested heavily in mapping its digital infrastructure and identifying critical assets and vulnerabilities. This proactive approach to understanding its digital "battlefield" was a part of a $250 million annual cybersecurity budget that included hiring 1,000 dedicated cybersecurity professionals (Krebs on Security, 2014). When the attackers attempted to infiltrate its systems, the bank's defenses, designed around its meticulously mapped digital terrain, successfully thwarted the breach. This incident underscores the indispensability of understanding one's digital landscape in safeguarding sensitive information.

Conclusion

In the digital age, where cyberthreats lurk around every corner, Sun Tzu's "Know Thyself" wisdom rings more accurate than ever. By understanding the foundations of your digital terrain, conducting regular cyber hygiene assessments, embracing a culture of continuous improvement, and harnessing the power of threat intelligence, you can strengthen your organization's cyber resilience and emerge victorious in the ever-evolving cyber battlefield.

As Sun Tzu himself proclaimed, "The supreme art of war is to subdue the enemy without fighting." Similarly, the ultimate victory in cybersecurity lies in securing your digital assets and preserving your organization's integrity and reputation without succumbing to the adversary's advances.

> "If your enemy is secure at all points, be prepared for him. If he is in superior strength, evade him. If your opponent is temperamental, seek to irritate him. Pretend to be weak, that he may grow arrogant. If he is taking his ease, give him no rest. If his forces are united, separate them. Attack him where he is unprepared; appear where you are not expected."
>
> — Sun Tzu, *The Art of War*

> If you fail to prepare, you have lost before you begin. Leaning forward into proactive measures before a cybersecurity incident is any organization's best defensive measure.
>
> — Jim West, Cybersecurity Expert

Chapter 3

Be Prepared

Preparation vs. Readiness

In cybersecurity, the concepts of being prepared and being ready are closely related but distinct. Each plays a crucial role in how organizations and individuals defend against threats. To fully appreciate their differences, it's helpful to explore these terms in the context of both strategic planning and real-time response.

Preparedness in cybersecurity refers to the state of having the necessary tools, strategies, and protocols in place before an attack occurs. It involves the proactive measures that an organization takes to anticipate potential threats and vulnerabilities. Being prepared is about building a robust defense through activities like conducting risk assessments, implementing security frameworks, establishing incident response plans, and ensuring regular training for staff.

For example, a prepared organization has likely conducted thorough vulnerability assessments, identified critical assets, and implemented strong security controls like firewalls, encryption, and multi-factor authentication. Preparedness also includes regular updates and patches to software and systems, ensuring known vulnerabilities are addressed before they can be exploited. Additionally, a prepared organization has invested in continuous monitoring tools to detect potential intrusions and has established clear protocols for responding to various types of incidents.

However, being ready in cybersecurity goes a step beyond preparedness. Readiness is about the ability to respond effectively when a cyber threat or attack actually occurs. It is the real-time application of the preparation efforts, the readiness to act swiftly and decisively when faced with an immediate threat. While preparedness is more about planning and prevention, readiness is about execution under pressure.

For instance, consider a scenario where a company experiences a ransomware attack. If the company is prepared, it will have backups, incident response plans, and a trained team in place. However, readiness is demonstrated when the team can quickly identify the attack, isolate affected systems, initiate the response plan, and communicate effectively internally and with stakeholders. It's the difference between having a plan and being able to execute that plan smoothly in a high-stress, real-time environment.

Readiness also involves adaptability. Cyberthreats evolve rapidly, and even the best-laid plans can face unforeseen challenges. Being ready means that an organization or individual is not only equipped to follow a plan but also to adapt that plan on the fly when new information emerges or when the situation changes. This might include adjusting response strategies, deploying additional resources, or making critical decisions with limited information.

Proactive Cybersecurity Measures

Sun Tzu's axiom, "Supreme excellence consists of breaking

the enemy's resistance without fighting," emphasizes the paramount importance of preparation and foresight in achieving victory. This principle, deeply ingrained in warfare, is equally critical in cybersecurity, where the landscape is fraught with ever-evolving threats and vulnerabilities. Winning the battle against cyberthreats necessitates a proactive stance, anticipating and neutralizing threats before they materialize into attacks.

Proactive Defense

In cybersecurity, a proactive defense strategy involves anticipating potential threats, understanding the adversary's tactics, and fortifying defenses accordingly. This approach requires continuous threat intelligence, vulnerability assessments, and implementing security best practices to mitigate risks before they can be exploited.

Proactive defense strategies can also include cyber deception, attribution, threat hunting, and adversarial pursuit.

Cultivating a Culture of Vigilance

To be prepared, we will classify vigilance under preparedness for its emphasis on sustained attention. Sun Tzu emphasizes the importance of discipline, vigilance, and adaptability in warfare. Similarly, fostering a culture of security awareness among employees is paramount in cybersecurity. Human error remains one of the weakest links in the cybersecurity chain, and educating personnel about the importance of adhering to security policies, recognizing phishing attempts, and exercising caution while handling sensitive information can significantly mitigate the risk of successful cyber-attacks.

Regular training sessions, simulated phishing exercises, and incident response drills empower employees to recognize and respond effectively to security threats, thereby bolstering the organization's overall cyber resilience.

Embracing a Culture of Continuous Improvement

Vigilance also comes with continuous learning and adaptation in the face of adversity. Similarly, in cybersecurity, organizations must embrace a culture of continuous improvement, staying abreast of emerging threats, evolving attack techniques, and best practices in defense. This ties well into the iterative process that already occurs with Strategic Thinking in Part One.

Case Studies

Being Prepared and Evading Superior Strength: The Google Aurora Attack

In 2009, Google was targeted by Operation Aurora, a sophisticated cyber-attack originating from China. The attackers aimed at accessing Gmail accounts of Chinese human rights activists, exploiting a vulnerability in Internet Explorer. Google's response was multifaceted, including enhancing their security infrastructure and publicly disclosing the attack, which not only raised awareness but also led to a broad industry push for better security practices. Importantly, Google shifted towards more secure computing platforms, moving away from Windows PCs for internal use to evade potential future attacks exploiting similar vulnerabilities (Wired, 2010).

The Estonian Cyber Defense Strategy

Following a series of coordinated cyber-attacks in 2007, which targeted Estonian government and private sector websites, Estonia became a global leader in cybersecurity by adopting a proactive and comprehensive national cyber defense strategy. Recognizing the necessity of preparation and resilience, Estonia established the NATO Cooperative Cyber Defence Centre of Excellence, invested heavily in cybersecurity education, and developed a robust national cyber incident response capability. Through these measures, Estonia has significantly enhanced its cyber resilience, effectively winning its cyber battles through diligent preparation and strategic foresight (NATO CCD COE, 2008).

Anticipating and Neutralizing Threats: The Microsoft Digital Crimes Unit

The Microsoft Digital Crimes Unit (DCU) exemplifies the principle of anticipating and neutralizing threats through its proactive measures against cybercrime. Leveraging advanced analytics and collaborating with law enforcement agencies worldwide, the DCU identifies and disrupts cybercrime operations before they can cause widespread harm. One notable success was the disruption of the Necurs botnet, one of the largest networks of infected computers, responsible for distributing malware and spam. Through strategic analysis and global collaboration, Microsoft was able to dismantle the botnet's infrastructure, effectively neutralizing a significant cyber threat before it could escalate (Microsoft On the Issues, 2020).

Building Resilience through Red Teaming: The Financial Sector's Embrace of Red Teaming

The financial sector, recognizing the critical importance of cybersecurity resilience, has widely adopted red teaming to bolster defenses. One illustrative example is the Bank of England's CBEST framework, which facilitates controlled, tailored, and realistic cyber-attack simulations on financial institutions. Through these exercises, banks and financial services firms can identify weaknesses in their cyber defenses and remediate them before real attackers can exploit them. This proactive approach to cybersecurity, aligning with Sun Tzu's teachings, ensures that financial institutions are prepared for and can withstand cyberthreats (Bank of England, 2016).

Conclusion

In summary, being prepared in cybersecurity is about laying the groundwork: having the tools, knowledge, and strategies in place to prevent and mitigate potential threats. It's a necessary foundation and part of the overall equation for success in the field.

Failing to prepare for potential attacks before they occur can have catastrophic consequences for an organization. When preparation is neglected, the response to an incident becomes reactive rather than proactive, leading to a host of challenges that can severely undermine the organization's ability to protect its digital assets, maintain operations, and preserve its reputation.

Without proper preparation, an organization lacks a clear understanding of its vulnerabilities, making it difficult to anticipate and mitigate potential threats. Preparation involves conducting risk assessments, identifying critical assets, and implementing security measures to protect them. Without these steps, the organization may not even know where its weaknesses lie, leaving it exposed to a wide range of cyberthreats. For example, unpatched systems, weak passwords, and misconfigured networks can serve as easy entry points for attackers. In the absence of preparation, these vulnerabilities remain unchecked, creating significant risks.

When a cyber-attack occurs in an unprepared organization, the lack of an established incident response plan exacerbates the situation. Incident response plans are critical for guiding actions during a cyber-attack, ensuring the organization can quickly contain and mitigate the damage. These plans outline roles and responsibilities, communication protocols, and specific steps to be taken in various scenarios. If no such plan exists, the organization will likely face confusion and disarray during an incident. Teams may not know who is responsible for critical decisions, communication may break down, and the response may be slow and ineffective, allowing the attack to spread and inflict more damage.

The absence of regular training and drills means that personnel are ill-equipped to recognize and respond to threats. Cybersecurity is not solely a technological issue; it also involves human factors. Employees who are not trained in cybersecurity best practices are more likely to fall victim to phishing schemes, inadvertently download malware, or otherwise compromise the organization's defenses. Moreover, without practicing incident response through drills and simulations, even the most well-crafted plans are likely to falter when put into action. In the heat of an actual incident, untrained personnel may panic, make errors, or fail to act swiftly, leading to a prolonged and more damaging attack.

Failing to prepare also means that the organization likely has inadequate monitoring and detection systems in place. Preparation includes setting up systems to detect and alert suspicious activities in real-time, enabling a swift response to emerging threats. Without these systems, an attack may go undetected for an extended period, allowing attackers to move laterally within the network, exfiltrate data, or cause other forms of harm. By the time the attack is discovered, the damage may be extensive and challenging to reverse.

The financial and reputational impact of such unpreparedness can be devastating. A successful cyber-attack can result in significant financial losses due to downtime, data breaches, legal penalties, and the cost of remediation. Furthermore, the loss of sensitive data—such as customer information or intellectual property—can erode trust and damage the organization's reputation, leading to a loss of business and long-term harm to its brand.

Neglecting to prepare for cybersecurity attacks before they occur sets the stage for chaos and failure during an incident. Without preparation, an organization is vulnerable to a wide range of threats, lacks a coordinated response, and is likely to suffer significant operational, financial, and reputational damage. Preparation is not merely a best practice in cybersecurity; it is an essential defense mechanism that enables organizations to anticipate, respond to, and recover from attacks effectively. Without it, the consequences can be dire, with far-reaching implications for the organization's future.

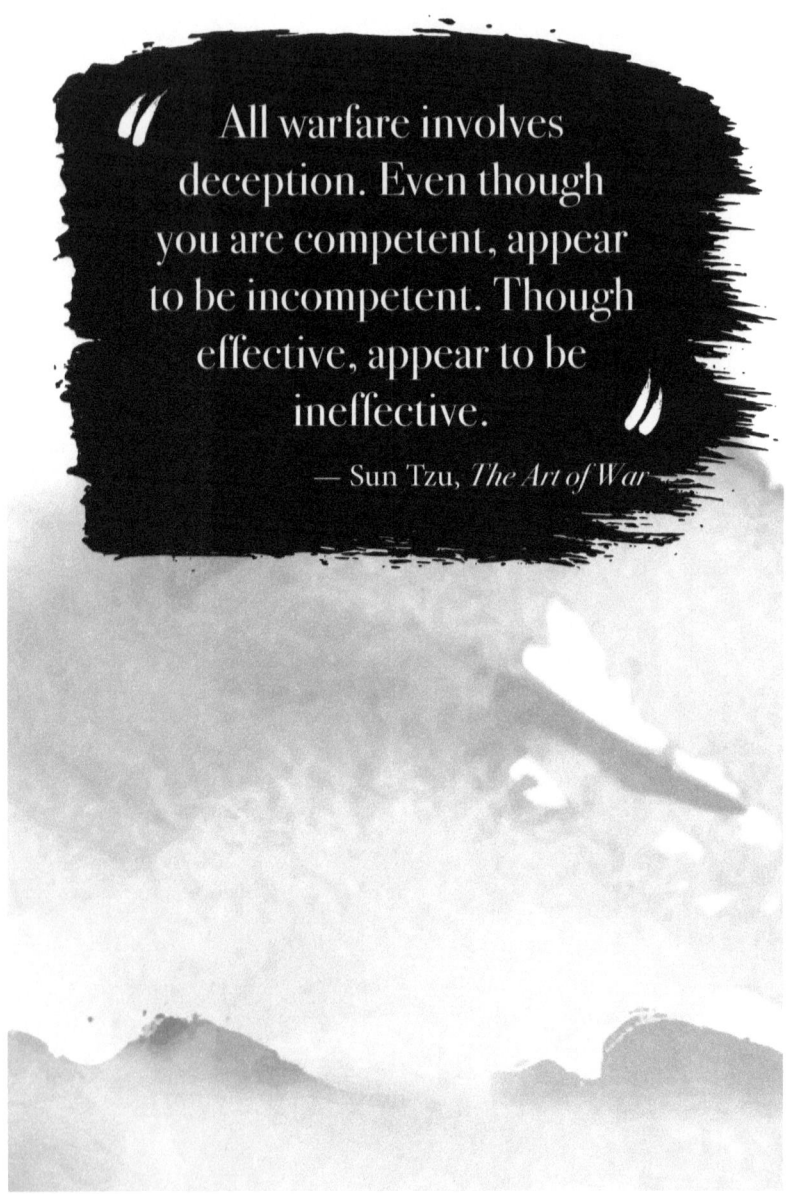

> *All warfare involves deception. Even though you are competent, appear to be incompetent. Though effective, appear to be ineffective.*
>
> — Sun Tzu, *The Art of War*

> Honeypots and Honeynets are best when they appear to be real systems. Attackers will gain access eventually, and it is best for them to go there than to the REAL systems.
>
> — Jim West, Cybersecurity Expert

Chapter 4

Be Deceptive

The Principle of Deception and Misdirection

Sun Tzu emphasizes using deception to outmaneuver adversaries and gain an advantage. In cybersecurity, this principle is applied through tactics such as honeypots, deceptive encryption, and red team operations. These methods lure attackers into traps, obscure critical assets, and simulate adversarial strategies, effectively disrupting and thwarting their objectives.

In the ever-evolving field of cybersecurity, where adversaries constantly seek to exploit vulnerabilities, mastering the art of deception is crucial for maintaining a defensive edge. This chapter delves into how organizations can integrate Sun Tzu's teachings into cybersecurity practices to confound attackers and strengthen their security posture.

Defining Deception

Deception, at its core, feels contradictory, where two things cannot be both true at the same time. According to the Oxford Dictionary, deception can involve the following tactics:

Dissimulation - the concealment of one's thoughts, feelings, or character.

Propaganda - information that is biased or misleading in nature to support a particular cause or point of view.

Distraction - prevents someone from giving full attention to something else or causes extreme agitation of the mind or emotions.

Camouflage/Concealment - to hide or disguise the presence of a person, place, or thing.

There is also self-deception, such as beguilement, deceit, bluff, mystification, ruse, or subterfuge. You'll notice that deception is also about seizing an opportunity, distorting the truth, and adapting quickly.

The Strategic Role of Deception in Cyber Defense

Sun Tzu's maxim highlights that deception is not merely a tactic but a strategic imperative in warfare. In cybersecurity, organizations must adopt a similar mindset, leveraging deception techniques to mislead and outmaneuver adversaries. By appearing weaker or less competent than they genuinely are, organizations can lure adversaries into complacency and exploit their overconfidence to gain an advantage.

Creating a Deceptive Cyber Environment

One effective way to implement Sun Tzu's principle of deception is to create a deceptive cyber environment. This may involve deploying honeypots, decoy systems, and false information to lure attackers and divert their attention away from critical assets. By presenting adversaries with enticing targets that appear vulnerable, organizations can entrap and gather intelligence on their adversaries' tactics, techniques, and procedures (TTPs), thereby strengthening their defenses and enhancing their situational awareness.

Cloaking Critical Assets and Deceptive Encryption

Sun Tzu's wisdom extends to the concept of appearing ineffective even when one is effective. Organizations can apply this principle in cybersecurity by employing deceptive encryption techniques to cloak critical assets and mislead adversaries. By encrypting decoy files or misleading data with false information using advanced cryptographic algorithms, organizations can obfuscate their actual assets and confuse adversaries attempting to exfiltrate sensitive information.

Fostering a Culture of Disinformation

In Sun Tzu's philosophy, deception is not limited to tactical maneuvers but permeates every aspect of warfare. Similarly, in cybersecurity, organizations can foster a culture of disinformation by strategically disseminating false or misleading information to adversaries. This may involve misleading indicators of compromise (IOCs), decoy credentials, or deceptive breadcrumbs designed to mislead and confuse attackers, thwarting their reconnaissance efforts and hindering their ability to execute successful cyber-attacks.

Case Studies

Deceptive Defense: The Use of Honeytokens

Honeytokens are a form of deception technology where fake data or tokens are interspersed with real data to mislead attackers. An illustrative example of this strategy was employed by a large e-commerce company that inserted fic-titious user records into its database. These records, if accessed or used, would trigger alerts to the security team, indicating a breach. In one in-stance, the company detected an insider threat when a malicious employee at-tempted to sell customer data on the dark web. The honeytokens allowed the company to quickly identify and neutral-ize the threat, showcasing the efficacy of appearing vulnerable to uncover and counteract malicious activities (Schneier on Security, 2017)

Pretending to Be Weak: Honey Pots

Honey pots have been effectively used by various organizations to lure cyber-attackers into revealing their tactics, techniques, and procedures. For instance, a major financial institution deployed a network of honey pots that mimicked vulnerable financial systems. Attackers, believing these to be easy targets, engaged with the honey pots, inadvertently exposing their methods to the institution's cybersecurity team. This intelligence allowed for the strengthening of actual defenses and the development of more effective countermeasures (Cybersecurity Insiders, 2019).

Misdirection and Waste: Confusing Attackers with Fake Networks

Another application of deception is the creation of entire fake networks, or honeypots, designed to mimic valuable targets. A notable example occurred when a government agency created a series of honeypots that simulated critical infrastructure systems. These honeypots were designed to be easily discoverable by attackers, drawing their attention away from real assets. When adversaries engaged with these decoy systems, they unwittingly revealed their methods, tools, and intentions. Furthermore, the time and resources they expended on these fruitless endeavors depleted their capabilities and provided defenders with valuable intelligence for strengthening actual defenses (Cybersecurity and Infrastructure Security Agency (CISA), 2019).

Operational Deception: Masking True Capabilities

A strategic approach to operational deception involves disguising the true state of system updates and patches. In one case, a financial institution faced persistent targeted attacks exploiting known vulnerabilities. In response, the institution accelerated its patching process but deliberately maintained the appearance of being slow to update its systems. This was achieved by selectively exposing vulnerabilities on systems isolated from critical networks, leading attackers to believe their exploits remained effective. As a result, attackers continued to use known exploits against these decoy systems, allowing the institution to monitor their activities without risking significant damage to its real assets (Financial Services Information Sharing and Analysis Center (FS-ISAC), 2020).

Conclusion

Sun Tzu's teachings on the strategic use of deception have profound relevance in cybersecurity. By manipulating attackers' perceptions through the appearance of incompetence or vulnerability, defenders can lead adversaries into traps, deplete their resources, and gain critical insights into their methods. Modern cybersecurity practices, such as the deployment of honeytokens, honeypots, and operational deception, exemplify these ancient strategies in action. In the ever-changing cyber battlefield, where the struggle between attackers and defenders is relentless, deception stands out as a powerful tool for protecting digital domains.

Sun Tzu's wisdom offers invaluable guidance for organizations aiming to bolster their cyber defenses and outmaneuver adversaries. By mastering the art of deception, organizations can strategically mislead and confound attackers, thereby strengthening their security measures and safeguarding their digital assets. As Sun Tzu wisely observed, "All warfare involves deception." By embracing this principle, organizations can gain the upper hand in cyber defense and successfully navigate the challenges posed by persistent and evolving threats.

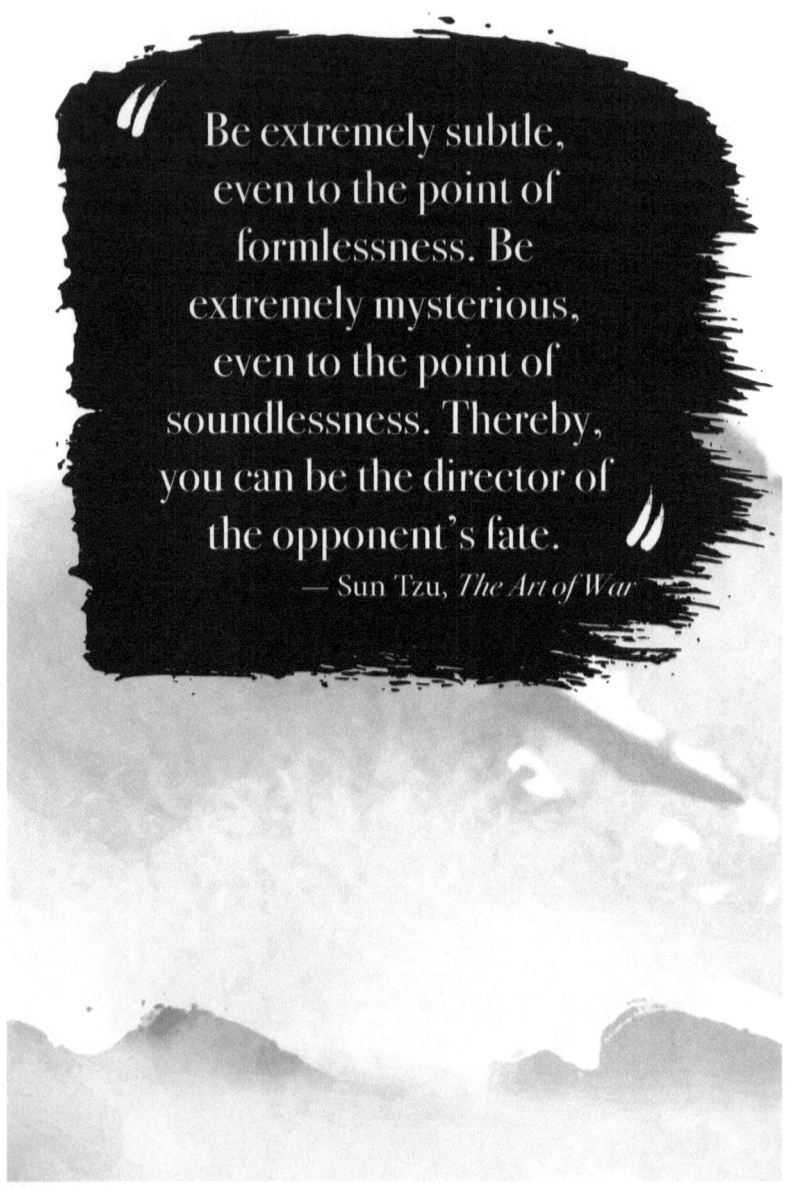

> "Be extremely subtle, even to the point of formlessness. Be extremely mysterious, even to the point of soundlessness. Thereby, you can be the director of the opponent's fate."
> — Sun Tzu, *The Art of War*

> It is simply unacceptable for any organization to not employ separation of duties, mandatory vacations, least privileges, and least functionality. Yet the most crucial is to review for effectiveness.
>
> — Jim West, Cybersecurity Expert

Chapter 5

Be Formless

Flexability in Strategy

In *The Art of War*, Sun Tzu states, "Let your plans be dark and impenetrable as night, and when you move, fall like a thunderbolt," epitomizing the strategic imperative of secrecy and decisive action in warfare. This principle holds profound significance in cybersecurity, where adversaries constantly probe defenses and exploit vulnerabilities. This chapter delves into how organizations can align Sun Tzu's teachings with cybersecurity principles to cloak their plans in secrecy and execute decisive actions with precision and impact.

Secrecy as a Strategic Advantage

Sun Tzu's directive to keep plans dark and impenetrable underscores the importance of maintaining operational secrecy in cybersecurity. Organizations must carefully conceal their intentions and strategies from adversaries, preventing them from anticipating and thwarting defensive measures. This involves limiting information disclosure, compartmentalizing operations, and implementing strict access controls to safeguard sensitive data and intelligence.

Agility and Adaptability in Response

Sun Tzu emphasizes the importance of agility and adaptability in responding to changing circumstances on the battlefield. In cybersecurity, this principle underscores the need for organizations to maintain flexibility and resilience in the face of evolving threats. By developing incident response plans, conducting tabletop exercises, and implementing agile security controls, organizations can rapidly detect, respond to, and recover from cyber incidents, minimizing the impact on their operations and reputation.

In Chapter 6 of the 1910 translation of *The Art of War*, Sun Tzu also discusses how it can be fatal to reuse tactics that may have worked in the past: "Do not repeat the tactics which have gained you one victory, but let your methods be regulated by the infinite variety of circumstances." Remaining flexible and resourceful means taking new developments or circumstances and leveraging them to your advantage.

Case Studies

The Role of Agility in Incident Response: The Garmin Ransomware Attack

A recent cybersecurity incident that highlights the importance of agility in an organization's response is the 2020 attack on Garmin, a well-known company that produces GPS devices and fitness trackers. Garmin's handling of this incident showcases how a quick, agile response can help mitigate damage and lead to a positive outcome.

In July 2020, Garmin was hit by a ransomware attack that

disrupted its services globally. The ransomware, identified as a variant of WastedLocker, encrypted Garmin's files and demanded a multi-million dollar ransom for their release. The attack caused significant outages, affecting Garmin's fitness tracking services, customer support, aviation database services, and even its production facilities.

Garmin's agile response to the ransomware attack allowed the company to minimize the impact of the attack on its operations and customers. By quickly containing the ransomware, maintaining transparent communication, and efficiently restoring services, Garmin was able to recover from the incident with relatively limited long-term damage. The company's ability to act decisively and adapt to the evolving situation demonstrated the importance of agility in incident response.

Advantage of Secrecy: The Stuxnet Worm

A notable cybersecurity incident that highlights secrecy as a strategic advantage is the 2010 Stuxnet attack. Stuxnet is widely regarded as one of the most sophisticated and secretive cyber operations ever conducted, and it has had a profound impact on the landscape of cybersecurity and cyber warfare.

Stuxnet was a highly advanced computer worm that targeted the industrial control systems (ICS) used in Iran's Natanz nuclear enrichment facility. The worm was designed specifically to infect Siemens PLCs (programmable logic controllers), which are commonly used to control machinery in industrial settings.

Once Stuxnet infiltrated the system, it altered the speed of the centrifuges used in uranium enrichment, causing them to spin at either too high or too low speeds, which ultimately led to the physical degradation of the centrifuges and disrupted Iran's nuclear program.

The strategic advantage of secrecy played a crucial role in the success of the Stuxnet operation. The creators of Stuxnet, believed to be a joint effort by the United States and Israel, went to great lengths to ensure that the worm remained undetected for as long as possible. The malware was meticulously designed to avoid detection by traditional cybersecurity measures (Wired, 2014).

Conclusion

In conclusion, the principles of secrecy, agility, and adaptability, as outlined by Sun Tzu and applied in contemporary cybersecurity, are critical for defending against the sophisticated and relentless threats that organizations face today. Garmin and Stuxnet's case studies underscore these strategies' power in real-world scenarios.

Garmin's swift and agile response to a ransomware attack exemplifies how adaptability and decisive action can mitigate damage and restore operations with minimal long-term impact. On the other hand, the Stuxnet incident highlights how strategic secrecy can be leveraged to carry out a highly effective and undetected operation, achieving significant objectives without immediate resistance.

These examples illustrate that in the digital battlefield, just as in traditional warfare, the ability to conceal intentions, respond quickly to changing threats, and adapt strategies as needed is paramount. Organizations that master these principles are better positioned to protect critical assets, outmaneuver adversaries, and maintain operational integrity. As Sun Tzu wisely advised, success in any conflict—whether on the physical battlefield or in cyberspace—depends on the careful orchestration of secrecy, strategy, and the agility to respond to unforeseen challenges with speed and precision. Much like how water takes the shape of the container it's held in, tactics must change to the circumstances that limit an organization.

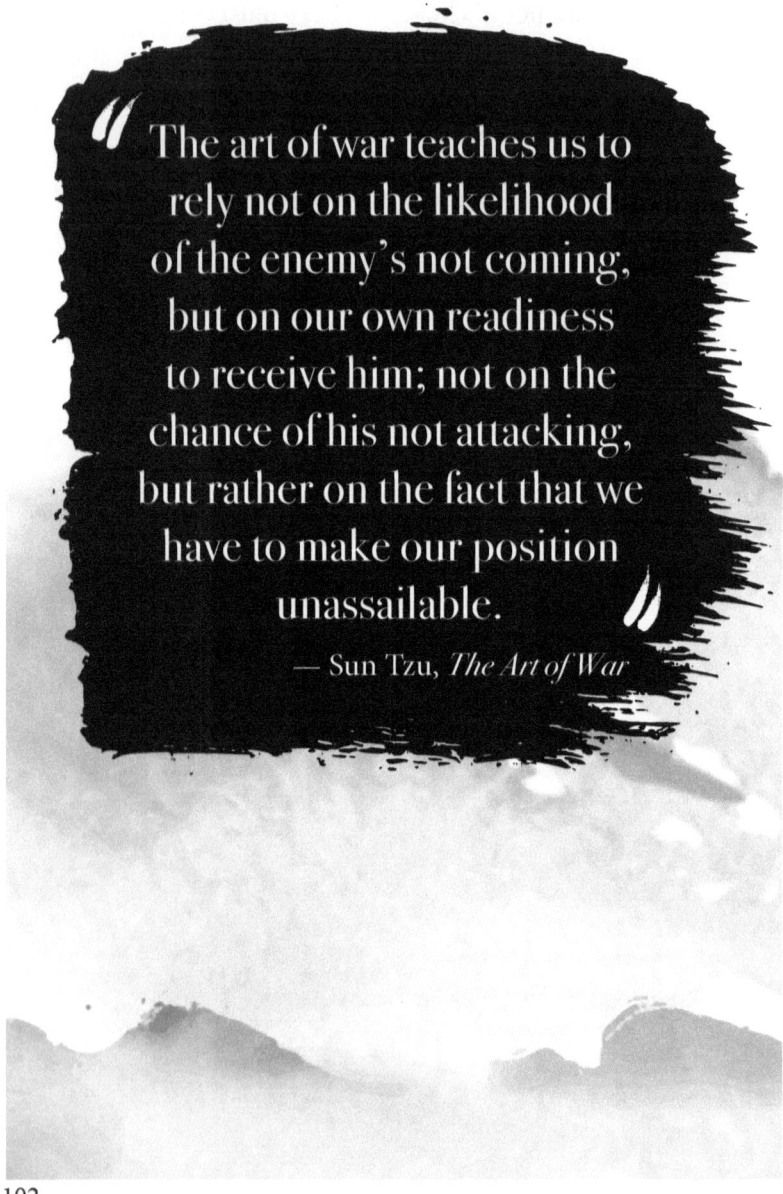

> "The art of war teaches us to rely not on the likelihood of the enemy's not coming, but on our own readiness to receive him; not on the chance of his not attacking, but rather on the fact that we have to make our position unassailable."
>
> — Sun Tzu, *The Art of War*

> It is inevitable that incidents will occur. How quickly, accurately, and complete it is handled is critical to recovery.
>
> — Jim West, Cybersecurity Expert

Chapter 6

Be Ready

Readiness and Adaptability

As we discussed, being ready in cybersecurity goes a step beyond preparedness. Readiness is about the ability to respond effectively when a cyber threat or attack actually occurs. This boils down to how quickly and accurately well-laid plans can be implemented in real-time. Remember: While preparedness is more about planning and prevention, readiness is about execution under pressure.

Readiness also involves adaptability. As discussed in Be Formless, cyberthreats evolve rapidly, and even the best-laid plans can face unforeseen challenges. Being ready means not only that an individual, team, department, or organization is equipped to follow a plan but also has the autonomy and knowledge to adapt that plan on the fly when new information emerges or when the situation changes. This might include adjusting response strategies, deploying additional resources, or making critical decisions with limited information and deferring back to one of the types of judgment we covered in Part One.

What Does Effective Adaptability Look Like?

Successful adaptability can sometimes be hard to find because when it's successful, it's ever-changing. Unlike a traditional snapshot, when a solution is adaptable, it keeps pace with changing priorities, projects, technologies, and environments.

The Pitfalls of AI Real-Time Monitoring

In some cases, AI has been pitched and positioned as a valuable tool to promote an organization's readiness. However, many may not understand that at the time of writing this, AI still faces challenges in grasping the overall context of what is occurring.

Sometimes, real-time response has its drawbacks. AI systems make the best decisions based on factors and variables, but it is often hard to put qualitative context into quantitative algorithms.

For example, it may deem an increase in traffic a DoS attack, and by trying to prevent the alleged DoS attack, it can inadvertently cut off legitimate traffic. In cutting off the legitimate traffic, the organization is dead in the water because the decision was made without the full context of business continuity needs.

Ensuring Readiness

Not surprisingly, a critical aspect of cybersecurity preparedness is the development and implementation of incident response plans. These plans outline procedures for detecting, responding to, and recovering from cyber incidents, ensuring that organizations can quickly and effectively mitigate damage.

Case Study

The Maersk NotPetya Recovery

When Maersk, the world's largest shipping company, was hit by the NotPetya ransomware, its operations were significantly disrupted. However, Maersk's effective incident response played a crucial role in its recovery. The company had an incident response plan that included backing up data and systems, which proved invaluable. Despite the severe initial impact, Maersk was able to restore its operations within 10 days, a feat that underscored the importance of preparedness and the presence of a solid incident response framework in cybersecurity (Wired, 2018).

Conclusion

The paramount importance of readiness cannot be overstated. At any level, cybersecurity professionals should advocate for a proactive approach to their strategies in the detection, response and planned recovery measures prior to an incident occurring.

Just as Sun Tzu's timeless wisdom underscores the necessity of knowing both the enemy and oneself, effective cybersecurity requires a deep understanding of potential threats and the dynamic fortification of defenses, ensuring resilience in the face of often relentless and sophisticated adversaries.

> "Let your plans be dark and impenetrable as night, and when you move, fall like a thunderbolt."
>
> — Sun Tzu, *The Art of War*

> The true power of speed lies in the accuracy of its execution. It is in the delicate balance between sound judgment and perfect timing that precision becomes paramount.
>
> — Jim West, Cybersecurity Expert

Chapter 7

Be Fast

Precision in Execution

When the time comes to act, Sun Tzu advises falling like a thunderbolt - swift, decisive, and overwhelming in force. He says, "The quality of decision is like the well-timed swoop of a falcon which enables it to strike and destroy its victim."
In cybersecurity, organizations must execute their defensive maneuvers with precision and speed, exploiting vulnerabilities and neutralizing threats before adversaries have a chance to react. This requires well-coordinated incident response teams, automated threat detection and response systems, and clear escalation procedures to ensure swift and effective action.

Leveraging Advanced Technologies

To achieve the level of precision and impact advocated by Sun Tzu, organizations must leverage advanced technologies to augment their cybersecurity capabilities. Artificial intelligence (AI), machine learning (ML), and predictive analytics can give organizations real-time insights into emerging threats and enable proactive defense measures. Additionally, technologies such as deception, endpoint detection and response (EDR), and threat-hunting platforms can enhance organizations' ability to detect and respond to cyberthreats with precision and efficiency.

Case Studies

The Swift Neutralization of WannaCry

The global WannaCry ransomware attack in May 2017 presented a critical test for cybersecurity teams worldwide. The malware spread rapidly, exploiting a vulnerability in Microsoft Windows systems. However, the attack was halted almost as swiftly as it began, thanks to the quick actions of cybersecurity researchers. One such researcher, operating under the pseudonym "MalwareTech," discovered and activated a "kill switch" in the malware's code, effectively stopping its spread. This rapid response exemplifies Sun Tzu's principle of striking decisively; by quickly understanding and acting upon the weakness in WannaCry's design, the researcher was able to mitigate a global cybersecurity crisis (BBC News, 2017).

Giving No Rest and Separating Forces: The DDoS Attacks on Financial Institutions

In 2012, a series of DDoS attacks targeted major U.S. banks, overwhelming their websites with traffic and disrupting services. The attacks were attributed to a state-sponsored group seeking to destabilize the financial sector. In response, banks increased their investment in DDoS mitigation technologies, improved their incident response protocols, and collaborated with law enforcement and other financial institutions to share threat intelligence. This collective defense strategy helped to isolate the attackers' capabilities and reduce the impact of subsequent DDoS campaigns (The New York Times, 2012).

Conclusion

Sun Tzu's wisdom on secrecy and decisive action offers invaluable insights for organizations seeking to enhance their cybersecurity capabilities and outmaneuver adversaries in the digital arena. By cloaking their plans in secrecy, executing with precision, leveraging advanced technologies, and adopting an agile and adaptive defense posture, organizations can unleash the thunderbolt of cyber warfare, striking fear into the hearts of adversaries and emerging victorious in the ongoing battle for digital supremacy.

Sun Tzu advises, "Let your plans be dark and impenetrable as night, and when you move, fall like a thunderbolt." By mastering the art of strategic precision, organizations can seize the initiative in cyber warfare and shape the future of digital security.

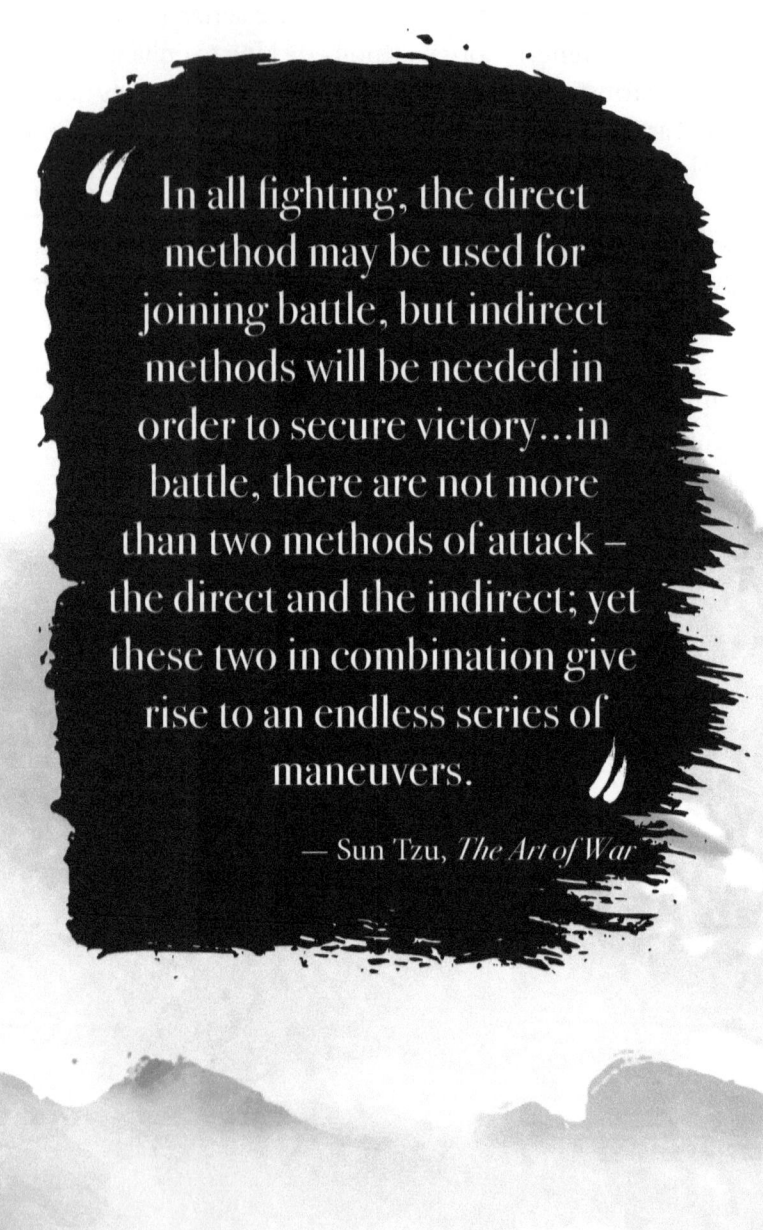

> In all fighting, the direct method may be used for joining battle, but indirect methods will be needed in order to secure victory…in battle, there are not more than two methods of attack – the direct and the indirect; yet these two in combination give rise to an endless series of maneuvers.

— Sun Tzu, *The Art of War*

> To find true success means to achieve mastery against the odds. Nothing is as binary as we hope for it to be because solutions will always incorporate a multitude of factors.
>
> — Jim West, Cybersecurity Expert

Chapter 8

Be Victorious

Winning the War

To be victorious, Sun Tzu advised long ago, "There is no instance of a country having benefited from prolonged warfare. It is only one who is thoroughly acquainted with the evils of war that can thoroughly understand the profitable way of carrying it on," which is why he cautions to be quick in the execution of conflict and always with the hope of avoiding war altogether.

Ways Leaders Have Failed

In the 1910 translation of *The Art of War*, in Chapter 8, Sun Tzu lists the five faults that can affect a general and lead them to ruin:

- Recklessness, which leads to destruction,
- Cowardice, which leads to capture,
- A hasty temper, which can be provoked by insults,
- A delicacy of honor, which is sensitive to shame,
- Over-solicitude for his men exposes him to worry and trouble.

Sun Tzu later covers what makes a victorious general: "The general who advances without coveting fame and retreats without fearing disgrace, whose only thought is to protect his country and do good service for his sovereign, is the jewel of the kingdom."

The best leaders know the terrain, know their army and know what difficulties they will face when weighing their actions. What I found quite interesting, though, was Sun Tzu's guidance that does, at times, directly contradict his ruler:

- If a ruler says not to fight, but a competent general sees that victory is clear, they should fight.
- If a ruler says to fight, but defeat is certain, then do not fight.
- A good general makes decisions without seeking fame or fearing blame.
- A leader cannot be confident if any factor of the battle is unsure.
- If the terrain is unclear, victory is not certain.
- If a leader does not know their soldiers, victory is not clear.
- A leader is confident in their movements, as any doubt can sow doubt in the troops.

This seems to be reinforced when he states, "The commander stands for the virtues of wisdom, sincerity, benevolence, courage, and strictness," with the not-so-subtle hints that sometimes what is best for a nation may not always align with the orders from its leadership.

Conclusion

It feels appropriate to close this chapter with one last "lofty ideal"—that of what a successful leader in cybersecurity embodies.

What a successful leader in cybersecurity looks like today is a blend of technical acumen, strategic vision, and interpersonal skills, all of which are critical to navigating the complex and ever-evolving landscape of digital threats. Such a leader is not only well-versed in the intricacies of cybersecurity technology but also understands the broader organizational and societal implications of security decisions. This person effectively balances the need for robust security measures with the organization's operational goals, ensuring that security does not become an obstacle but rather a facilitator of innovation and growth.

At the core of their leadership is a deep understanding of risk management. They recognize that absolute security is unattainable and instead focus on prioritizing resources to protect the most critical assets. This involves continuously assessing the threat landscape, anticipating emerging risks, and adapting strategies accordingly. A successful cybersecurity leader is proactive, not reactive, identifying potential vulnerabilities before they can be exploited and implementing preventative and responsive measures.

Communication is another pivotal aspect of their role. They must articulate complex technical issues in a way that is accessible to non-technical stakeholders, including executive leadership, board members, and other departments. This ability to translate technical jargon into business language is crucial for securing the necessary support and resources for cybersecurity initiatives. Moreover, they foster a culture of security awareness across the organization, ensuring that all employees understand their role in maintaining security, from following best practices to reporting suspicious activities.

Collaboration is also essential. Cybersecurity is not the responsibility of a single individual or department but requires coordinated efforts across the organization. A successful leader builds strong relationships with other departments, understanding their unique challenges and working together to integrate security into every aspect of the business. They also maintain external partnerships, keeping the organization connected with the broader cybersecurity community, sharing intelligence, and staying ahead of the latest threats.

Moreover, ethical considerations guide their leadership. Cybersecurity leaders are often faced with difficult decisions that have significant implications for privacy, trust, and the ethical use of data. They must weigh the potential benefits of specific actions against the possible consequences for individuals and society at large, ensuring that their decisions align with both legal requirements and moral principles.

Finally, a successful cybersecurity leader is adaptable and continuously learning. The cybersecurity field is characterized by rapid change, with new threats and technologies emerging at an unprecedented pace. Leaders in this space must stay current with the latest developments, continually enhancing their knowledge and skills and fostering a culture of learning within their teams. They encourage innovation and experimenting with new approaches and technologies while also being ready to pivot when circumstances change.

In summary, a successful leader in cybersecurity is a multidimensional figure, adept at managing risks, communicating effectively, fostering collaboration, upholding ethical standards, and remaining agile in the face of change. Their leadership ensures that the organization not only defends against threats but also leverages cybersecurity as a competitive advantage in an increasingly digital world.

My hope now, as you move on to Part Three, is that you'll

continue to see how interwoven these concepts of effective leadership truly are. While perfection is not obtainable, the desire to continue learning and push toward perpetual improvement is what defines success.

Final Remarks

Embracing Timeless Wisdom

As we reach the culmination of our exploration of Sun Tzu's *The Art of War* and its profound relevance to modern cybersecurity, we find ourselves in awe of the enduring wisdom embedded within this ancient text. The strategic insights it offers transcend the traditional confines of warfare, illuminating a path forward for those engaged in the silent, yet no less consequential, battles of the digital age.

Each chapter of this timeless work reveals a deeper truth—principles of preparation, knowledge, deception, agility, and the art of non-confrontational victory—that resonate powerfully within the complex, ever-evolving landscape of cybersecurity. Though articulated over two millennia ago, these tenets remain strikingly applicable, guiding today's professionals in their sacred duty to protect and preserve the digital frontiers of our world from the ever-present, ever-evolving threats that seek to undermine them.

Sun Tzu's profound teachings remind us that true victory is born from a deep understanding of both our enemies and ourselves. In the realm of cybersecurity, this requires perpetual learning and adaptation—a continuous sharpening of our knowledge of potential threats and a candid assessment of our own vulnerabilities. Through the countless examples we have encountered, we have witnessed how organizations that embody Sun Tzu's counsel—foreseeing attacks, neutralizing threats without direct confrontation, and employing stealth and surprise—are those that rise to meet the challenges of the cyber battlefield with resilience and strength.

Sun Tzu's emphasis on preparation and strategic foresight—on winning the battle before it is ever fought—resonates with profound clarity in cybersecurity. The proactive measures so critical to safeguarding digital spaces, from building robust defenses to conducting red teaming exercises, mirror Sun Tzu's call to make one's position unassailable. It is this preparedness that serves as a fortress, standing tall against the persistent and cunning adversaries who seek to breach our digital walls.

The art of deception, a central theme in *The Art of War*, teaches us the power of misdirection and the value of surprise, both of which are indispensable in cybersecurity. The strategic deployment of honeypots and the adoption of the zero-trust model allow organizations to obscure their defenses, ensnaring attackers in traps while gathering intelligence to turn against them. These tactics, forged in the crucible of Sun Tzu's ancient wisdom, not only protect vital assets but transform our defenses into an active force capable of neutralizing threats with minimal confrontation.

Yet perhaps the most profound lesson that Sun Tzu imparts to us is the supreme art of subduing the enemy without fighting—of securing victory through non-confrontational means. This principle lies at the very heart of cybersecurity's ultimate goal: to create a digital environment so fortified and resilient that would-be attackers are dissuaded from attempting their schemes, knowing that their efforts are destined to fail. In this, Sun Tzu offers us not merely a strategy, but a vision of security so complete, so harmonious, that conflict itself is rendered unnecessary.

In sum, Sun Tzu's *The Art of War* provides us with a blueprint for strategic thought and action that is as vital to the cyber conflicts of today as it was to the military struggles of the ancient world. The pillars of understanding, preparation, deception, and non-confrontation form the foundation of effective cybersecurity strategies, offering timeless guidance in an age where the stakes are as high as ever. As we navigate the intricate terrain of the digital battlefield, Sun Tzu's wisdom remains a beacon of clarity and strength, guiding us toward victory in the unseen wars of the 21st century.

Part Three

The Art of War

The Art of War by Sun Tzu

In this section, I've included Lionel Giles' 1910 translation of *The Art of War*. There are at least eight modern translations of the original 13 letters Sun Tzu wrote. Still, it's important to note there are always biases built into any individual who writes the translation and what time in history they're writing from. These invisible influences are very real and shape the final product they produce, much like history itself.

Giles' translation is now part of the Public Domain. In the United States, this means his translated work is no longer subject to copyright and can be reprinted and reproduced.

I felt it was essential to include a copy of *The Art of War* in this work so that you, dear reader, can digest it yourself and find your own insights to take with you moving forward. Over the years, I've found that as I've experienced more, what I take away each time I read varies and expands greatly.

So, I encourage you to revisit it every year or so, reread it, and let it soak into more of your daily work and operations.

Chapter 1

Laying Plans

1. Sun Tzu said: The art of war is of vital importance to the State.

2. It is a matter of life and death, a road either to safety or to ruin. Hence it is a subject of inquiry which can on no account be neglected.

3. The art of war, then, is governed by five constant factors, to be taken into account in one's deliberations, when seeking to determine the conditions obtaining in the field.

4. These are:

> (1) The Moral Law;
>
> (2) Heaven;
>
> (3) Earth;
>
> (4) The Commander;
>
> (5) Method and discipline.

5. The MORAL LAW causes the people to be in complete accord with their ruler, so that they will follow him regardless of their lives, undismayed by any danger.

6. HEAVEN signifies night and day, cold and heat, times and seasons.

7. EARTH comprises distances, great and small; danger and security; open ground and narrow passes; the chances of life and death.

8. The COMMANDER stands for the virtues of wisdom, sincerity, benevolence, courage and strictness.

9. By METHOD AND DISCIPLINE are to be understood the marshaling of the army in its proper subdivisions, the graduations of rank among the officers, the maintenance of roads by which supplies may reach the army, and the control of military expenditure.

10. These five heads should be familiar to every general: he who knows them will be victorious; he who knows them not will fail.

11. Therefore, in your deliberations, when seeking to determine the military conditions, let them be made the basis of a comparison, in this wise: –

> 12. (1) Which of the two sovereigns is imbued with the Moral law?
>
> (2) Which of the two generals has most ability?
>
> (3) With whom lie the advantages derived from Heaven and Earth? (4) On which side is discipline most rigorously enforced?
>
> (5) Which army is stronger?
>
> (6) On which side are officers and men more highly trained?
>
> (7) In which army is there the greater constancy both in reward and punishment?

13. By means of these seven considerations I can forecast victory or defeat.

14. The general that hearkens to my counsel and acts upon it, will conquer: —let such a one be retained in command! The general that hearkens not to my counsel nor acts upon it, will suffer defeat: —let such a one be dismissed!

15. While heeding the profit of my counsel, avail yourself also of any helpful circumstances over and beyond the ordinary rules.

16. According as circumstances are favorable, one should modify one's plans.

17. All warfare is based on deception.

18. Hence, when able to attack, we must seem unable; when using our forces, we must seem inactive; when we are near, we must make the enemy believe we are far away; when far away, we must make him believe we are near.

19. Hold out baits to entice the enemy. Feign disorder, and crush him.

20. If he is secure at all points, be prepared for him. If he is in superior strength, evade him.

21. If your opponent is of choleric temper, seek to irritate him. Pretend to be weak, that he may grow arrogant.

22. If he is taking his ease, give him no rest. If his forces are united, separate them.

23. Attack him where he is unprepared, appear where you are not expected.

24. These military devices, leading to victory, must not be divulged beforehand.

25. Now the general who wins a battle makes many calculations in his temple ere the battle is fought. The general who loses a battle makes but few calculations beforehand. Thus do many

calculations lead to victory, and few calculations to defeat: how much more no calculation at all! It is by attention to this point that I can foresee who is likely to win or lose.

Chapter 2

Waging War

1. Sun Tzu said: In the operations of war, where there are in the field a thousand swift chariots, as many heavy chariots, and a hundred thousand mail-clad soldiers, with provisions enough to carry them a thousand LI, the expenditure at home and at the front, including entertainment of guests, small items such as glue and paint, and sums spent on chariots and armor, will reach the total of a thousand ounces of silver per day. Such is the cost of raising an army of 100,000 men.

2. When you engage in actual fighting, if victory is long in coming, then men's weapons will grow dull and their ardor will be damped. If you lay siege to a town, you will exhaust your strength.

3. Again, if the campaign is protracted, the resources of the State will not be equal to the strain.

4. Now, when your weapons are dulled, your ardor damped, your strength exhausted and your treasure spent, other chieftains will spring up to take advantage of your extremity. Then no man, however wise, will be able to avert the consequences that must ensue.

5. Thus, though we have heard of stupid haste in war, cleverness has never been seen associated with long delays.

6. There is no instance of a country having benefited from prolonged warfare.

7. It is only one who is thoroughly acquainted with the evils of war that can thoroughly understand the profitable way of carrying it on.

8. The skillful soldier does not raise a second levy, neither are his supply-wagons loaded more than twice.

9. Bring war material with you from home, but forage on the enemy. Thus the army will have food enough for its needs.

10. Poverty of the State exchequer causes an army to be maintained by contributions from a distance. Contributing to maintain an army at a distance causes the people to be impoverished.

11. On the other hand, the proximity of an army causes prices to go up; and high prices cause the people's substance to be drained away.

12. When their substance is drained away, the peasantry will be afflicted by heavy exactions.

13. With this loss of substance and exhaustion of strength, the homes of the people will be stripped bare, and three-tenths of their income will be dissipated; while government expenses for broken chariots, worn-out horses, breast-plates and helmets, bows and arrows, spears and shields, protective mantles, draught-oxen and heavy wagons, will amount to four-tenths of its total revenue.

14. Hence a wise general makes a point of foraging on the enemy. One cartload of the enemy's provisions is equivalent to twenty of one's own, and likewise a single PICUL of his provender is equivalent to twenty from one's own store.

15. Now in order to kill the enemy, our men must be roused to anger; that there may be advantage from defeating the enemy, they must have their rewards.

16. Therefore in chariot fighting, when ten or more chariots have been taken, those should be rewarded who took the first. Our own flags should be substituted for those of the enemy, and the chariots mingled and used in conjunction with ours. The captured soldiers should be kindly treated and kept.

17. This is called, using the conquered foe to augment one's own strength.

18. In war, then, let your great object be victory, not lengthy campaigns.

19. Thus it may be known that the leader of armies is the arbiter of the people's fate, the man on whom it depends whether the nation shall be in peace or in peril.

Chapter 3

Attack by Stratagem

1. Sun Tzu said: In the practical art of war, the best thing of all is to take the enemy's country whole and intact; to shatter and destroy it is not so good. So, too, it is better to recapture an army entire than to destroy it, to capture a regiment, a detachment or a company entire than to destroy them.

2. Hence to fight and conquer in all your battles is not supreme excellence; supreme excellence consists in breaking the enemy's resistance without fighting.

3. Thus the highest form of generalship is to balk the enemy's plans; the next best is to prevent the junction of the enemy's forces; the next in order is to attack the enemy's army in the field; and the worst policy of all is to besiege walled cities.

4. The rule is, not to besiege walled cities if it can possibly be avoided. The preparation of mantlets, movable shelters, and various implements of war, will take up three whole months; and the piling up of mounds over against the walls will take three months more.

5. The general, unable to control his irritation, will launch his men to the assault like swarming ants, with the result that one-third of his men are slain, while the town still remains untaken. Such are the disastrous effects of a siege.

6. Therefore the skillful leader subdues the enemy's troops without any fighting; he captures their cities without laying siege to them; he overthrows their kingdom without lengthy operations in the field.

7. With his forces intact he will dispute the mastery of the Empire, and thus, without losing a man, his triumph will be complete. This is the method of attacking by stratagem.

8. It is the rule in war, if our forces are ten to the enemy's one, to surround him; if five to one, to attack him; if twice as numerous, to divide our army into two.

9. If equally matched, we can offer battle; if slightly inferior in numbers, we can avoid the enemy; if quite unequal in every way, we can flee from him.

10. Hence, though an obstinate fight may be made by a small force, in the end it must be captured by the larger force.

11. Now the general is the bulwark of the State; if the bulwark is complete at all points; the State will be strong; if the bulwark is defective, the State will be weak.

12. There are three ways in which a ruler can bring misfortune upon his army:—

> 13. (1) By commanding the army to advance or to retreat, being ignorant of the fact that it cannot obey. This is called hobbling the army.

> 14. (2) By attempting to govern an army in the same way as he administers a kingdom, being ignorant of the conditions which obtain in an army. This causes restlessness in the soldier's minds.

> 15. (3) By employing the officers of his army without discrimination, through ignorance of the military principle of

adaptation to circumstances. This shakes the confidence of the soldiers.

16. But when the army is restless and distrustful, trouble is sure to come from the other feudal princes. This is simply bringing anarchy into the army, and flinging victory away.

17. Thus we may know that there are five essentials for victory:

> (1) He will win who knows when to fight and when not to fight.

> (2) He will win who knows how to handle both superior and inferior forces.

> (3) He will win whose army is animated by the same spirit throughout all its ranks.

> (4) He will win who, prepared himself, waits to take the enemy unprepared.

> (5) He will win who has military capacity and is not interfered with by the sovereign.

18. Hence the saying: If you know the enemy and know yourself, you need not fear the result of a hundred battles. If you know yourself but not the enemy, for every victory gained you will also suffer a defeat. If you know neither the enemy nor yourself, you will succumb in every battle.

Chapter 4

Tactical Dispositions

1. Sun Tzu said: The good fighters of old first put themselves beyond the possibility of defeat, and then waited for an opportunity of defeating the enemy.

2. To secure ourselves against defeat lies in our own hands, but the opportunity of defeating the enemy is provided by the enemy himself.

3. Thus the good fighter is able to secure himself against defeat, but cannot make certain of defeating the enemy.

4. Hence the saying: One may KNOW how to conquer without being able to DO it.

5. Security against defeat implies defensive tactics; ability to defeat the enemy means taking the offensive.

6. Standing on the defensive indicates insufficient strength; attacking, a superabundance of strength.

7. The general who is skilled in defense hides in the most secret recesses of the earth; he who is skilled in attack flashes forth from the topmost heights of heaven. Thus on the one hand we have ability to protect ourselves; on the other, a victory that is complete.

8. To see victory only when it is within the ken of the common herd is not the acme of excellence.

9. Neither is it the acme of excellence if you fight and conquer and the whole Empire says, "Well done!"

10. To lift an autumn hair is no sign of great strength; to see the sun and moon is no sign of sharp sight; to hear the noise of thunder is no sign of a quick ear.

11. What the ancients called a clever fighter is one who not only wins, but excels in winning with ease.

12. Hence his victories bring him neither reputation for wisdom nor credit for courage.

13. He wins his battles by making no mistakes. Making no mistakes is what establishes the certainty of victory, for it means conquering an enemy that is already defeated.

14. Hence the skillful fighter puts himself into a position which makes defeat impossible, and does not miss the moment for defeating the enemy.

15. Thus it is that in war the victorious strategist only seeks battle after the victory has been won, whereas he who is destined to defeat first fights and afterwards looks for victory.

16. The consummate leader cultivates the moral law, and strictly adheres to method and discipline; thus it is in his power to control success.

17. In respect of military method, we have, firstly, Measurement; secondly, Estimation of quantity; thirdly, Calculation; fourthly, Balancing of chances; fifthly, Victory.

18. Measurement owes its existence to Earth; Estimation of quantity to Measurement; Calculation to Estimation of quantity; Balancing of chances to Calculation; and Victory to Balancing of chances.

19. A victorious army opposed to a routed one, is as a pound's weight placed in the scale against a single grain.

20. The onrush of a conquering force is like the bursting of pent-up waters into a chasm a thousand fathoms deep.

Chapter 5

Energy

1. Sun Tzu said: The control of a large force is the same principle as the control of a few men: it is merely a question of dividing up their numbers.

2. Fighting with a large army under your command is nowise different from fighting with a small one: it is merely a question of instituting signs and signals.

3. To ensure that your whole host may withstand the brunt of the enemy's attack and remain unshaken - this is effected by maneuvers direct and indirect.

4. That the impact of your army may be like a grindstone dashed against an egg - this is effected by the science of weak points and strong.

5. In all fighting, the direct method may be used for joining battle, but indirect methods will be needed in order to secure victory.

6. Indirect tactics, efficiently applied, are inexhaustible as Heaven and Earth, unending as the flow of rivers and streams; like the sun and moon, they end but to begin anew; like the four seasons, they pass away to return once more.

7. There are not more than five musical notes, yet the combinations of these five give rise to more melodies than can ever be heard.

8. There are not more than five primary colors (blue, yellow, red, white, and black), yet in combination they produce more hues than can ever been seen.

9. There are not more than five cardinal tastes (sour, acrid, salt, sweet, bitter), yet combinations of them yield more flavors than can ever be tasted.

10. In battle, there are not more than two methods of attack - the direct and the indirect; yet these two in combination give rise to an endless series of maneuvers.

11. The direct and the indirect lead on to each other in turn. It is like moving in a circle - you never come to an end. Who can exhaust the possibilities of their combination?

12. The onset of troops is like the rush of a torrent which will even roll stones along in its course.

13. The quality of decision is like the well-timed swoop of a falcon which enables it to strike and destroy its victim.

14. Therefore the good fighter will be terrible in his onset, and prompt in his decision.

15. Energy may be likened to the bending of a crossbow; decision, to the releasing of a trigger.

16. Amid the turmoil and tumult of battle, there may be seeming disorder and yet no real disorder at all; amid confusion and chaos, your array may be without head or tail, yet it will be proof against defeat.

17. Simulated disorder postulates perfect discipline, simulated fear postulates courage; simulated weakness postulates strength.

18. Hiding order beneath the cloak of disorder is simply a question of subdivision; concealing courage under a show of

timidity presupposes a fund of latent energy; masking strength with weakness is to be effected by tactical dispositions.

19. Thus one who is skillful at keeping the enemy on the move maintains deceitful appearances, according to which the enemy will act. He sacrifices something, that the enemy may snatch at it.

20. By holding out baits, he keeps him on the march; then with a body of picked men he lies in wait for him.

21. The clever combatant looks to the effect of combined energy, and does not require too much from individuals. Hence his ability to pick out the right men and utilize combined energy.

22. When he utilizes combined energy, his fighting men become as it were like unto rolling logs or stones. For it is the nature of a log or stone to remain motionless on level ground, and to move when on a slope; if four-cornered, to come to a standstill, but if round-shaped, to go rolling down.

23. Thus the energy developed by good fighting men is as the momentum of a round stone rolled down a mountain thousands of feet in height. So much on the subject of energy.

Chapter 6

Attack by Stratagem

1. Sun Tzu said: Whoever is first in the field and awaits the coming of the enemy, will be fresh for the fight; whoever is second in the field and has to hasten to battle will arrive exhausted.

2. Therefore the clever combatant imposes his will on the enemy, but does not allow the enemy's will to be imposed on him.

3. By holding out advantages to him, he can cause the enemy to approach of his own accord; or, by inflicting damage, he can make it impossible for the enemy to draw near.

4. If the enemy is taking his ease, he can harass him; if well supplied with food, he can starve him out; if quietly encamped, he can force him to move.

5. Appear at points which the enemy must hasten to defend; march swiftly to places where you are not expected.

6. An army may march great distances without distress, if it marches through country where the enemy is not.

7. You can be sure of succeeding in your attacks if you only attack places which are undefended. You can ensure the safety of your defense if you only hold positions that cannot be attacked.

8. Hence that general is skillful in attack whose opponent does not know what to defend; and he is skillful in defense whose opponent does not know what to attack.

9. O divine art of subtlety and secrecy! Through you we learn to be invisible, through you inaudible; and hence we can hold the enemy's fate in our hands.

10. You may advance and be absolutely irresistible, if you make for the enemy's weak points; you may retire and be safe from pursuit if your movements are more rapid than those of the enemy.

11. If we wish to fight, the enemy can be forced to an engagement even though he be sheltered behind a high rampart and a deep ditch. All we need do is attack some other place that he will be obliged to relieve.

12. If we do not wish to fight, we can prevent the enemy from engaging us even though the lines of our encampment be merely traced out on the ground. All we need do is to throw something odd and unaccountable in his way.

13. By discovering the enemy's dispositions and remaining invisible ourselves, we can keep our forces concentrated, while the enemy's must be divided.

14. We can form a single united body, while the enemy must split up into fractions. Hence there will be a whole pitted against separate parts of a whole, which means that we shall be many to the enemy's few.

15. And if we are able thus to attack an inferior force with a superior one, our opponents will be in dire straits.

16. The spot where we intend to fight must not be made known; for then the enemy will have to prepare against a possible attack at several different points; and his forces being thus distributed

in many directions, the numbers we shall have to face at any given point will be proportionately few.

17. For should the enemy strengthen his van, he will weaken his rear; should he strengthen his rear, he will weaken his van; should he strengthen his left, he will weaken his right; should he strengthen his right, he will weaken his left. If he sends reinforcements everywhere, he will everywhere be weak.

18. Numerical weakness comes from having to prepare against possible attacks; numerical strength, from compelling our adversary to make these preparations against us.

19. Knowing the place and the time of the coming battle, we may concentrate from the greatest distances in order to fight.

20. But if neither time nor place be known, then the left wing will be impotent to succor the right, the right equally impotent to succor the left, the van unable to relieve the rear, or the rear to support the van. How much more so if the furthest portions of the army are anything under a hundred LI apart, and even the nearest are separated by several LI!

21. Though according to my estimate the soldiers of Yueh exceed our own in number, that shall advantage them nothing in the matter of victory. I say then that victory can be achieved.

22. Though the enemy be stronger in numbers, we may prevent him from fighting. Scheme so as to discover his plans and the likelihood of their success.

23. Rouse him, and learn the principle of his activity or inactivity. Force him to reveal himself, so as to find out his vulnerable spots.

24. Carefully compare the opposing army with your own, so that you may know where strength is superabundant and where it is deficient.

25. In making tactical dispositions, the highest pitch you can attain is to conceal them; conceal your dispositions, and you will be safe from the prying of the subtlest spies, from the machinations of the wisest brains.

26. How victory may be produced for them out of the enemy's own tactics—that is what the multitude cannot comprehend.

27. All men can see the tactics whereby I conquer, but what none can see is the strategy out of which victory is evolved.

28. Do not repeat the tactics which have gained you one victory, but let your methods be regulated by the infinite variety of circumstances.

29. Military tactics are like unto water; for water in its natural course runs away from high places and hastens downwards.

30. So in war, the way is to avoid what is strong and to strike at what is weak.

31. Water shapes its course according to the nature of the ground over which it flows; the soldier works out his victory in relation to the foe whom he is facing.

32. Therefore, just as water retains no constant shape, so in warfare there are no constant conditions.

33. He who can modify his tactics in relation to his opponent and thereby succeed in winning, may be called a heaven-born captain.

34. The five elements (water, fire, wood, metal, earth) are not always equally predominant; the four seasons make way for each other in turn. There are short days and long; the moon has its periods of waning and waxing.

Chapter 7

Maneuvering

1. Sun Tzu said: In war, the general receives his commands from the sovereign.

2. Having collected an army and concentrated his forces, he must blend and harmonize the different elements thereof before pitching his camp.

3. After that, comes tactical maneuvering, than which there is nothing more difficult. The difficulty of tactical maneuvering consists in turning the devious into the direct, and misfortune into gain.

4. Thus, to take a long and circuitous route, after enticing the enemy out of the way, and though starting after him, to contrive to reach the goal before him, shows knowledge of the artifice of DEVIATION.

5. Maneuvering with an army is advantageous; with an undisciplined multitude, most dangerous.

6. If you set a fully equipped army in march in order to snatch an advantage, the chances are that you will be too late. On the other hand, to detach a flying column for the purpose involves the sacrifice of its baggage and stores.

7. Thus, if you order your men to roll up their buff-coats, and make forced marches without halting day or night, covering double the usual distance at a stretch, doing a hundred LI

in order to wrest an advantage, the leaders of all your three divisions will fall into the hands of the enemy.

8. The stronger men will be in front, the jaded ones will fall behind, and on this plan only one-tenth of your army will reach its destination.

9. If you march fifty LI in order to outmaneuver the enemy, you will lose the leader of your first division, and only half your force will reach the goal.

10. If you march thirty LI with the same object, two-thirds of your army will arrive.

11. We may take it then that an army without its baggage-train is lost; without provisions it is lost; without bases of supply it is lost.

12. We cannot enter into alliances until we are acquainted with the designs of our neighbors.

13. We are not fit to lead an army on the march unless we are familiar with the face of the country—its mountains and forests, its pitfalls and precipices, its marshes and swamps.

14. We shall be unable to turn natural advantage to account unless we make use of local guides.

15. In war, practice dissimulation, and you will succeed.

16. Whether to concentrate or to divide your troops, must be decided by circumstances.

17. Let your rapidity be that of the wind, your compactness that of the forest.

18. In raiding and plundering be like fire, in immovability like a mountain.

19. Let your plans be dark and impenetrable as night, and when you move, fall like a thunderbolt.

20. When you plunder a countryside, let the spoil be divided amongst your men; when you capture new territory, cut it up into allotments for the benefit of the soldiery.

21. Ponder and deliberate before you make a move.

22. He will conquer who has learnt the artifice of deviation. Such is the art of maneuvering.

23. The Book of Army Management says: On the field of battle, the spoken word does not carry far enough: hence the institution of gongs and drums. Nor can ordinary objects be seen clearly enough: hence the institution of banners and flags.

24. Gongs and drums, banners and flags, are means whereby the ears and eyes of the host may be focused on one particular point.

25. The host thus forming a single united body, it is impossible either for the brave to advance alone, or for the cowardly to retreat alone. This is the art of handling large masses of men.

26. In night-fighting, then, make much use of signal-fires and drums, and in fighting by day, of flags and banners, as a means of influencing the ears and eyes of your army.

27. A whole army may be robbed of its spirit; a commander-in-chief may be robbed of his presence of mind.

28. Now a soldier's spirit is keenest in the morning; by noonday it has begun to flag; and in the evening, his mind is bent only on returning to camp.

29. A clever general, therefore, avoids an army when its spirit is keen, but attacks it when it is sluggish and inclined to return. This is the art of studying moods.

30. Disciplined and calm, to await the appearance of disorder and hubbub amongst the enemy:—this is the art of retaining self-possession.

31. To be near the goal while the enemy is still far from it, to wait at ease while the enemy is toiling and struggling, to be well-fed while the enemy is famished:—this is the art of husbanding one's strength.

32. To refrain from intercepting an enemy whose banners are in perfect order, to refrain from attacking an army drawn up in calm and confident array:—this is the art of studying circumstances.

33. It is a military axiom not to advance uphill against the enemy, nor to oppose him when he comes downhill.

34. Do not pursue an enemy who simulates flight; do not attack soldiers whose temper is keen.

35. Do not swallow bait offered by the enemy. Do not interfere with an army that is returning home.

36. When you surround an army, leave an outlet free. Do not press a desperate foe too hard.

37. Such is the art of warfare.

Chapter 8

Variation in Tactics

1. Sun Tzu said: In war, the general receives his commands from the sovereign, collects his army and concentrates his forces.

2. When in difficult country, do not encamp. In country where high roads intersect, join hands with your allies. Do not linger in dangerously isolated positions. In hemmed-in situations, you must resort to stratagem. In desperate position, you must fight.

3. There are roads which must not be followed, armies which must be not attacked, towns which must not be besieged, positions which must not be contested, commands of the sovereign which must not be obeyed.

4. The general who thoroughly understands the advantages that accompany variation of tactics knows how to handle his troops.

5. The general who does not understand these, may be well acquainted with the configuration of the country, yet he will not be able to turn his knowledge to practical account.

6. So, the student of war who is unversed in the art of war of varying his plans, even though he be acquainted with the Five Advantages, will fail to make the best use of his men.

7. Hence in the wise leader's plans, considerations of advantage

and of disadvantage will be blended together.

8. If our expectation of advantage be tempered in this way, we may succeed in accomplishing the essential part of our schemes.

9. If, on the other hand, in the midst of difficulties we are always ready to seize an advantage, we may extricate ourselves from misfortune.

10. Reduce the hostile chiefs by inflicting damage on them; and make trouble for them, and keep them constantly engaged; hold out specious allurements, and make them rush to any given point.

11. The art of war teaches us to rely not on the likelihood of the enemy's not coming, but on our own readiness to receive him; not on the chance of his not attacking, but rather on the fact that we have made our position unassailable.

12. There are five dangerous faults which may affect a general:

> (1) Recklessness, which leads to destruction;

> (2) cowardice, which leads to capture;

> (3) a hasty temper, which can be provoked by insults;

> (4) a delicacy of honor which is sensitive to shame;

> (5) over-solicitude for his men, which exposes him to worry and trouble.

13. These are the five besetting sins of a general, ruinous to the conduct of war.

14. When an army is overthrown and its leader slain, the cause will surely be found among these five dangerous faults. Let them be a subject of meditation.

Chapter 9

The Army on the March

1. Sun Tzu said: We come now to the question of encamping the army, and observing signs of the enemy. Pass quickly over mountains, and keep in the neighborhood of valleys.

2. Camp in high places, facing the sun. Do not clumb heights in order to fight. So much for mountain warfare.

3. After crossing a river, you should get far away from it.

4. When an invating force crosses a river in its onward march, do not advance to meet it in mid-stream. It will be best to let half the army get across, and then deliver your attack.

5. If you are anxious to fight, you should not go to meet the invader near a river which he has to cross.

6. Moor your craft higher up than the enemy, and facing the sun. Do not move up-stream to meet the enemy. So much for the river warfare.

7. In crossing salt-marshes, your sole concern should be to get over them quickly, without any delay.

8. If forced to fight in a salt-marsh, you should have water and grass near you, and get your back to a clump of trees. So much for operations in salt-marches.

9. In dry, level country, take up an easily accessible position with rising ground to your right and on your rear, so that the danger may be in front, and safety lie behind. So much for campaigning in flat country.

10. These are the four useful branches of military knowledge which enabled the Yellow Emperor to vanquish four several sovereigns.

11. All armies prefer high ground to low and sunny places to dark.

12. If you are careful of your men, and camp on hard ground, the army will be free from diseases of every kind, and this will spell victory.

13. When you come to a hill or a bank, occupy the sunny side, with the slope on your right rear. Thus you will once act for the benefit of your soliders and utilize the natural advantages of the ground.

14. When, in consequence of heavy rains up-country, a river which you wish to ford is swollen and flecked with foam, you must wait until it subsides.

15. Country in which there are precipitous cliffs with torrents running between, deep natural hollows, confined placed, tangled thickets, quagmires and crevasses, should be left with all possible speed and not approached.

16. While we keep away from such places, we should get the enemy to approach them; while we face them, we shoudl let the enemy have them on his rear.

17. If in the neighborhood of your camp there should be an yhilly country, ponds surrounded by aquatic grass, hollow basins filled with reeds, or woods with thick undergrowth, they must be carefully routed out and searched; for these are placed where

men in ambush or insidious spies are likely to be lurking.

18. When the enemy is close at hand and remains quiet, he is relying on the natural strength of his position.

19. When he keeps aloof and tires to provoke a battle, he is anxious for the other side to advance.

20. If his place of encampment is eassy of access, he is tendering a bait.

21. Movement amongst the trees of a forest shows that the enemy is advancing. The appearance of a number of screens in the midst of thick grass means that the enemy wants to make us suspiscious.

22. The rising of birds in their flight is the sign of an ambuscade. Startled beasts indicate that a sudden attack is coming.

23. When there is dust rising in a high column, it is the sign of chariots advancing; when the dust is low, but spread over a wide area, it betokens the approach of infantry. When it branches out in different directions, it shows that parties have been sent to collect firewood. A few clouds of dust moving to and fro signify that the arm is encamping.

24. Humble words and increased preparations are signs that the enemy is about to advance. Violent language and driving forward as if to the attack are signs that he will retreat.

25. When the light chariots come out first and take up a position on the wings, it is a sign that the enemy is forming for battle.

26. Peace proposals unaccompanied by a sworn covenant indicate a plot.

27. When there is much running about and the soldiers fall into rank, it means that the critical moment has come.

28. When some are seen advancing and some retreating, it is a lure.

29. When the soldiers stand leaning on their spears, they are faint from want of food.

30. If those who are sent to draw water begin by drinking themselves, the army is suffering from thirst.

31. If the enemy sees an advantage to be gained and makes no effort to secure it, the soldiers are exhausted.

32. If birds gather on any spot, it is unoccupied. Clamor by night betokens nervousness.

33. If there is disturbance in the camp, the general's authority is weak. If the banners and flags are shifted about, sedition is afoot. If the officers are angry, it means that the men are weary.

34. When an army feeds its horses with grain and kills its cattle for food, and when the men do not hang their cooking-pots over the camp-fires, showing that they will not return to their tents, you may know that they are determined to fight to the death.

35. The sight of men whispering together in small knots or speaking in subdued tones points to disaffection amongst the rank and file.

36. Too frequent rewards signify that the enemy is at the end of his resources; too many punishments betray a condition of dire distress.

37. To begin by bluster, but afterwards to take fright at the enemy's numbers, shows a supreme lack of intelligence.

38. When envoys are sent with compliments in their mouths, it is a sign that the enemy wishes for a truce.

39. If the enemy's troops march up angrily and remain facing

ours for a long time without either joining battle or taking themselves off again, the situation is one that demands great vigilance and circumspection.

40. If our troops are no more in number than the enemy, that is amply sufficient; it only means that no direct attack can be made. What we can do is simply to concentrate all our available strength, keep a close watch on the enemy, and obtain reinforcements.

41. He who exercises no forethought but makes light of his opponents is sure to be captured by them.

42. If soldiers are punished before they have grown attached to you, they will not prove submissive; and, unless submissive, then will be practically useless. If, when the soldiers have become attached to you, punishments are not enforced, they will still be useless.

43. Therefore soldiers must be treated in the first instance with humanity, but kept under control by means of iron discipline. This is a certain road to victory.

44. If in training soldiers commands are habitually enforced, the army will be well-disciplined; if not, its discipline will be bad.

45. If a general shows confidence in his men but always insists on his orders being obeyed, the gain will be mutual.

Chapter 10

Terrain

1. Sun Tzu said: We may distinguish six kinds of terrain, to wit:

   (1) Accessible ground;

   (2) entangling ground;

   (3) temporizing ground;

   (4) narrow passes;

   (5) precipitous heights;

   (6) positions at a great distance from the enemy.

2. Ground which can be freely traversed by both sides is called ACCESSIBLE.

3. With regard to ground of this nature, be before the enemy in occupying the raised and sunny spots, and carefully guard your line of supplies. Then you will be able to fight with advantage.

4. Ground which can be abandoned but is hard to re-occupy is called ENTANGLING.

5. From a position of this sort, if the enemy is unprepared, you may sally forth and defeat him. But if the enemy is prepared for your coming, and you fail to defeat him, then, return being

impossible, disaster will ensue.

6. When the position is such that neither side will gain by making the first move, it is called TEMPORIZING ground.

7. In a position of this sort, even though the enemy should offer us an attractive bait, it will be advisable not to stir forth, but rather to retreat, thus enticing the enemy in his turn; then, when part of his army has come out, we may deliver our attack with advantage.

8. With regard to NARROW PASSES, if you can occupy them first, let them be strongly garrisoned and await the advent of the enemy.

9. Should the army forestall you in occupying a pass, do not go after him if the pass is fully garrisoned, but only if it is weakly garrisoned.

10. With regard to PRECIPITOUS HEIGHTS, if you are beforehand with your adversary, you should occupy the raised and sunny spots, and there wait for him to come up.

11. If the enemy has occupied them before you, do not follow him, but retreat and try to entice him away.

12. If you are situated at a great distance from the enemy, and the strength of the two armies is equal, it is not easy to provoke a battle, and fighting will be to your disadvantage.

13. These six are the principles connected with Earth. The general who has attained a responsible post must be careful to study them.

14. Now an army is exposed to six several calamities, not arising from natural causes, but from faults for which the general is responsible. These are:

(1) flight;

(2) insubordination;

(3) collapse;

(4) ruin;

(5) disorganization;

(6) rout.

15. Other conditions being equal, if one force is hurled against another ten times its size, the result will be the FLIGHT of the former.

16. When the common soldiers are too strong and their officers too weak, the result is INSUBORDINATION. When the officers are too strong and the common soldiers too weak, the result is COLLAPSE.

17. When the higher officers are angry and insubordinate, and on meeting the enemy give battle on their own account from a feeling of resentment, before the commander-in-chief can tell whether or not he is in a position to fight, the result is RUIN.

18. When the general is weak and without authority; when his orders are not clear and distinct; when there are no fixed duties assigned to officers and men, and the ranks are formed in a slovenly haphazard manner, the result is utter DISORGANIZATION.

19. When a general, unable to estimate the enemy's strength, allows an inferior force to engage a larger one, or hurls a weak detachment against a powerful one, and neglects to place picked soldiers in the front rank, the result must be ROUT.

20. These are six ways of courting defeat, which must be carefully noted by the general who has attained a responsible post.

21. The natural formation of the country is the soldier's best ally; but a power of estimating the adversary, of controlling the forces of victory, and of shrewdly calculating difficulties, dangers and distances, constitutes the test of a great general.

22. He who knows these things, and in fighting puts his knowledge into practice, will win his battles. He who knows them not, nor practices them, will surely be defeated.

23. If fighting is sure to result in victory, then you must fight, even though the ruler forbid it; if fighting will not result in victory, then you must not fight even at the ruler's bidding.

24. The general who advances without coveting fame and retreats without fearing disgrace, whose only thought is to protect his country and do good service for his sovereign, is the jewel of the kingdom.

25. Regard your soldiers as your children, and they will follow you into the deepest valleys; look upon them as your own beloved sons, and they will stand by you even unto death.

26. If, however, you are indulgent, but unable to make your authority felt; kind-hearted, but unable to enforce your commands; and incapable, moreover, of quelling disorder: then your soldiers must be likened to spoilt children; they are useless for any practical purpose.

27. If we know that our own men are in a condition to attack, but are unaware that the enemy is not open to attack, we have gone only halfway towards victory.

28. If we know that the enemy is open to attack, but are unaware that our own men are not in a condition to attack, we have gone only halfway towards victory.

29. If we know that the enemy is open to attack, and also know that our men are in a condition to attack, but are unaware that

the nature of the ground makes fighting impracticable, we have still gone only halfway towards victory.

30. Hence the experienced soldier, once in motion, is never bewildered; once he has broken camp, he is never at a loss.

31. Hence the saying: If you know the enemy and know yourself, your victory will not stand in doubt; if you know Heaven and know Earth, you may make your victory complete.

Chapter 11

The Nine Situations

1. Sun Tzu said: The art of war recognizes nine varieties of ground:

> (1) Dispersive ground;
>
> (2) facile ground;
>
> (3) contentious ground;
>
> (4) open ground;
>
> (5) ground of intersecting highways;
>
> (6) serious ground;
>
> (7) difficult ground;
>
> (8) hemmed-in ground;
>
> (9) desperate ground.

2. When a chieftain is fighting in his own territory, it is dispersive ground.

3. When he has penetrated into hostile territory, but to no great distance, it is facile ground.

4. Ground the possession of which imports great advantage to either side, is contentious ground.

5. Ground on which each side has liberty of movement is open

ground.

6. Ground which forms the key to three contiguous states, so that he who occupies it first has most of the Empire at his command, is a ground of intersecting highways.

7. When an army has penetrated into the heart of a hostile country, leaving a number of fortified cities in its rear, it is serious ground.

8. Mountain forests, rugged steeps, marshes and fens—all country that is hard to traverse: this is difficult ground.

9. Ground which is reached through narrow gorges, and from which we can only retire by tortuous paths, so that a small number of the enemy would suffice to crush a large body of our men: this is hemmed in ground.

10. Ground on which we can only be saved from destruction by fighting without delay, is desperate ground.

11. On dispersive ground, therefore, fight not. On facile ground, halt not. On contentious ground, attack not.

12. On open ground, do not try to block the enemy's way. On the ground of intersecting highways, join hands with your allies.

13. On serious ground, gather in plunder. In difficult ground, keep steadily on the march.

14. On hemmed-in ground, resort to stratagem. On desperate ground, fight.

15. Those who were called skillful leaders of old knew how to drive a wedge between the enemy's front and rear; to prevent co-operation between his large and small divisions; to hinder the good troops from rescuing the bad, the officers from rallying their men.

16. When the enemy's men were united, they managed to keep them in disorder.

17. When it was to their advantage, they made a forward move; when otherwise, they stopped still.

18. If asked how to cope with a great host of the enemy in orderly array and on the point of marching to the attack, I should say: "Begin by seizing something which your opponent holds dear; then he will be amenable to your will."

19. Rapidity is the essence of war: take advantage of the enemy's unreadiness, make your way by unexpected routes, and attack unguarded spots.

20. The following are the principles to be observed by an invading force: The further you penetrate into a country, the greater will be the solidarity of your troops, and thus the defenders will not prevail against you.

21. Make forays in fertile country in order to supply your army with food.

22. Carefully study the well-being of your men, and do not overtax them. Concentrate your energy and hoard your strength. Keep your army continually on the move, and devise unfathomable plans.

23. Throw your soldiers into positions whence there is no escape, and they will prefer death to flight. If they will face death, there is nothing they may not achieve. Officers and men alike will put forth their uttermost strength.

24. Soldiers when in desperate straits lose the sense of fear. If there is no place of refuge, they will stand firm. If they are in hostile country, they will show a stubborn front. If there is no help for it, they will fight hard.

25. Thus, without waiting to be marshaled, the soldiers will be constantly on the qui vive; without waiting to be asked, they will do your will; without restrictions, they will be faithful; without giving orders, they can be trusted.

26. Prohibit the taking of omens, and do away with superstitious doubts. Then, until death itself comes, no calamity need be feared.

27. If our soldiers are not overburdened with money, it is not because they have a distaste for riches; if their lives are not unduly long, it is not because they are disinclined to longevity.

28. On the day they are ordered out to battle, your soldiers may weep, those sitting up bedewing their garments, and those lying down letting the tears run down their cheeks. But let them once be brought to bay, and they will display the courage of a Chu or a Kuei.

29. The skillful tactician may be likened to the SHUAI-JAN. Now the SHUAI-JAN is a snake that is found in the Ch`ang mountains. Strike at its head, and you will be attacked by its tail; strike at its tail, and you will be attacked by its head; strike at its middle, and you will be attacked by head and tail both.

30. Asked if an army can be made to imitate the SHUAI-JAN, I should answer, Yes. For the men of Wu and the men of Yueh are enemies; yet if they are crossing a river in the same boat and are caught by a storm, they will come to each other's assistance just as the left hand helps the right.

31. Hence it is not enough to put one's trust in the tethering of horses, and the burying of chariot wheels in the ground.

32. The principle on which to manage an army is to set up one standard of courage which all must reach.

33. How to make the best of both strong and weak—that is a

question involving the proper use of ground.

34. Thus the skillful general conducts his army just as though he were leading a single man, willy-nilly, by the hand.

35. It is the business of a general to be quiet and thus ensure secrecy; upright and just, and thus maintain order.

36. He must be able to mystify his officers and men by false reports and appearances, and thus keep them in total ignorance.

37. By altering his arrangements and changing his plans, he keeps the enemy without definite knowledge. By shifting his camp and taking circuitous routes, he prevents the enemy from anticipating his purpose.

38. At the critical moment, the leader of an army acts like one who has climbed up a height and then kicks away the ladder behind him. He carries his men deep into hostile territory before he shows his hand.

39. He burns his boats and breaks his cooking-pots; like a shepherd driving a flock of sheep, he drives his men this way and that, and nothing knows whither he is going.

40. To muster his host and bring it into danger:—this may be termed the business of the general.

41. The different measures suited to the nine varieties of ground; the expediency of aggressive or defensive tactics; and the fundamental laws of human nature: these are things that must most certainly be studied.

42. When invading hostile territory, the general principle is, that penetrating deeply brings cohesion; penetrating but a short way means dispersion.

43. When you leave your own country behind, and take your

army across neighborhood territory, you find yourself on critical ground. When there are means of communication on all four sides, the ground is one of intersecting highways.

44. When you penetrate deeply into a country, it is serious ground. When you penetrate but a little way, it is facile ground.

45. When you have the enemy's strongholds on your rear, and narrow passes in front, it is hemmed-in ground. When there is no place of refuge at all, it is desperate ground.

46. Therefore, on dispersive ground, I would inspire my men with unity of purpose. On facile ground, I would see that there is close connection between all parts of my army.

47. On contentious ground, I would hurry up my rear.

48. On open ground, I would keep a vigilant eye on my defenses. On ground of intersecting highways, I would consolidate my alliances.

49. On serious ground, I would try to ensure a continuous stream of supplies. On difficult ground, I would keep pushing on along the road.

50. On hemmed-in ground, I would block any way of retreat. On desperate ground, I would proclaim to my soldiers the hopelessness of saving their lives.

51. For it is the soldier's disposition to offer an obstinate resistance when surrounded, to fight hard when he cannot help himself, and to obey promptly when he has fallen into danger.

52. We cannot enter into alliance with neighboring princes until we are acquainted with their designs. We are not fit to lead an army on the march unless we are familiar with the face of the country—its mountains and forests, its pitfalls and precipices, its marshes and swamps. We shall be unable to turn natural

advantages to account unless we make use of local guides.

53. To be ignored of any one of the following four or five principles does not befit a warlike prince.

54. When a warlike prince attacks a powerful state, his generalship shows itself in preventing the concentration of the enemy's forces. He overawes his opponents, and their allies are prevented from joining against him.

55. Hence he does not strive to ally himself with all and sundry, nor does he foster the power of other states. He carries out his own secret designs, keeping his antagonists in awe. Thus he is able to capture their cities and overthrow their kingdoms.

56. Bestow rewards without regard to rule, issue orders without regard to previous arrangements; and you will be able to handle a whole army as though you had to do with but a single man.

57. Confront your soldiers with the deed itself; never let them know your design. When the outlook is bright, bring it before their eyes; but tell them nothing when the situation is gloomy.

58. Place your army in deadly peril, and it will survive; plunge it into desperate straits, and it will come off in safety.

59. For it is precisely when a force has fallen into harm's way that is capable of striking a blow for victory.

60. Success in warfare is gained by carefully accommodating ourselves to the enemy's purpose.

61. By persistently hanging on the enemy's flank, we shall succeed in the long run in killing the commander-in-chief.

62. This is called ability to accomplish a thing by sheer cunning.

63. On the day that you take up your command, block the frontier passes, destroy the official tallies, and stop the passage

of all emissaries.

64. Be stern in the council-chamber, so that you may control the situation.

65. If the enemy leaves a door open, you must rush in.

66. Forestall your opponent by seizing what he holds dear, and subtly contrive to time his arrival on the ground.

67. Walk in the path defined by rule, and accommodate yourself to the enemy until you can fight a decisive battle.

68. At first, then, exhibit the coyness of a maiden, until the enemy gives you an opening; afterwards emulate the rapidity of a running hare, and it will be too late for the enemy to oppose you.

Chapter 12

The Attack by Fire

1. Sun Tzu said: There are five ways of attacking with fire. The first is to burn soldiers in their camp; the second is to burn stores; the third is to burn baggage trains; the fourth is to burn arsenals and magazines; the fifth is to hurl dropping fire amongst the enemy.

2. In order to carry out an attack, we must have means available. The material for raising fire should always be kept in readiness.

3. There is a proper season for making attacks with fire, and special days for starting a conflagration.

4. The proper season is when the weather is very dry; the special days are those when the moon is in the constellations of the Sieve, the Wall, the Wing or the Cross-bar; for these four are all days of rising wind.

5. In attacking with fire, one should be prepared to meet five possible developments:

6. (1) When fire breaks out inside to enemy's camp, respond at once with an attack from without.

7. (2) If there is an outbreak of fire, but the enemy's soldiers remain quiet, bide your time and do not attack.

8. (3) When the force of the flames has reached its height, follow it up with an attack, if that is practicable; if not, stay where you are.

9. (4) If it is possible to make an assault with fire from without, do not wait for it to break out within, but deliver your attack at a favorable moment.

10. (5) When you start a fire, be to windward of it. Do not attack from the leeward.

11. A wind that rises in the daytime lasts long, but a night breeze soon falls.

12. In every army, the five developments connected with fire must be known, the movements of the stars calculated, and a watch kept for the proper days.

13. Hence those who use fire as an aid to the attack show intelligence; those who use water as an aid to the attack gain an accession of strength.

14. By means of water, an enemy may be intercepted, but not robbed of all his belongings.

15. Unhappy is the fate of one who tries to win his battles and succeed in his attacks without cultivating the spirit of enterprise; for the result is waste of time and general stagnation.

16. Hence the saying: The enlightened ruler lays his plans well ahead; the good general cultivates his resources.

17. Move not unless you see an advantage; use not your troops unless there is something to be gained; fight not unless the position is critical.

18. No ruler should put troops into the field merely to gratify his own spleen; no general should fight a battle simply out of pique.

19. If it is to your advantage, make a forward move; if not, stay where you are.

20. Anger may in time change to gladness; vexation may be succeeded by content.

21. But a kingdom that has once been destroyed can never come again into being; nor can the dead ever be brought back to life.

22. Hence the enlightened ruler is heedful, and the good general full of caution. This is the way to keep a country at peace and an army intact.

Chapter 13

The Use of Spies

1. Sun Tzu said: Raising a host of a hundred thousand men and marching them great distances entails heavy loss on the people and a drain on the resources of the State. The daily expenditure will amount to a thousand ounces of silver. There will be commotion at home and abroad, and men will drop down exhausted on the highways. As many as seven hundred thousand families will be impeded in their labor.

2. Hostile armies may face each other for years, striving for the victory which is decided in a single day. This being so, to remain in ignorance of the enemy's condition simply because one grudges the outlay of a hundred ounces of silver in honors and emoluments, is the height of inhumanity.

3. One who acts thus is no leader of men, no present help to his sovereign, no master of victory.

4. Thus, what enables the wise sovereign and the good general to strike and conquer, and achieve things beyond the reach of ordinary men, is FOREKNOWLEDGE.

5. Now this foreknowledge cannot be elicited from spirits; it cannot be obtained inductively from experience, nor by any deductive calculation.

6. Knowledge of the enemy's dispositions can only be obtained from other men.

7. Hence the use of spies, of whom there are five classes:

    (1) Local spies;

    (2) inward spies;

    (3) converted spies;

    (4) doomed spies;

    (5) surviving spies.

8. When these five kinds of spy are all at work, none can discover the secret system. This is called "divine manipulation of the threads." It is the sovereign's most precious faculty.

9. Having LOCAL SPIES means employing the services of the inhabitants of a district.

10. Having INWARD SPIES, making use of officials of the enemy.

11. Having CONVERTED SPIES, getting hold of the enemy's spies and using them for our own purposes.

12. Having DOOMED SPIES, doing certain things openly for purposes of deception, and allowing our spies to know of them and report them to the enemy.

13. SURVIVING SPIES, finally, are those who bring back news from the enemy's camp.

14. Hence it is that which none in the whole army are more intimate relations to be maintained than with spies. None should be more liberally rewarded. In no other business should greater secrecy be preserved.

15. Spies cannot be usefully employed without a certain intuitive sagacity.

16. They cannot be properly managed without benevolence and straightforwardness.

17. Without subtle ingenuity of mind, one cannot make certain of the truth of their reports.

18. Be subtle! be subtle! and use your spies for every kind of business.

19. If a secret piece of news is divulged by a spy before the time is ripe, he must be put to death together with the man to whom the secret was told.

20. Whether the object be to crush an army, to storm a city, or to assassinate an individual, it is always necessary to begin by finding out the names of the attendants, the aides-de-camp, and door-keepers and sentries of the general in command. Our spies must be commissioned to ascertain these.

21. The enemy's spies who have come to spy on us must be sought out, tempted with bribes, led away and comfortably housed. Thus they will become converted spies and available for our service.

22. It is through the information brought by the converted spy that we are able to acquire and employ local and inward spies.

23. It is owing to his information, again, that we can cause the doomed spy to carry false tidings to the enemy.

24. Lastly, it is by his information that the surviving spy can be used on appointed occasions.

25. The end and aim of spying in all its five varieties is knowledge of the enemy; and this knowledge can only be

derived, in the first instance, from the converted spy. Hence it is essential that the converted spy be treated with the utmost liberality.

26. Of old, the rise of the Yin dynasty was due to I Chih who had served under the Hsia. Likewise, the rise of the Chou dynasty was due to Lu Ya who had served under the Yin.

27. Hence it is only the enlightened ruler and the wise general who will use the highest intelligence of the army for purposes of spying and thereby they achieve great results. Spies are a most important element in war, because on them depends an army's ability to move.

About the Author

Jim West is a distinguished figure in cybersecurity, known for his profound expertise and significant contributions to the discipline's academic and practical aspects. With over three decades of experience in the field, West has established himself as a leading authority on cybersecurity, information assurance, and digital forensics.

West's academic credentials include a Bachelor's in Cybersecurity and Information Security with his illustrious career. His educational journey is complemented by numerous professional certifications that are highly regarded in the cybersecurity community, including Certified Information Systems Security Professional (CISSP), Certified Ethical Hacker (CEH), and Certified Information Security Manager (CISM), among others.

Over the years, West has held various pivotal roles across a broad spectrum of organizations, ranging from consulting to Fortune 500 companies to government agencies. His career began in the trenches of IT operations, where he garnered hands-on experience in network administration and systems engineering. This practical experience, coupled with his academic background, provided West with a comprehensive understanding of the cybersecurity challenges organizations face.

As a cybersecurity strategist, West has designed and implemented robust security frameworks that safeguard digital assets against evolving threats. His work has significantly contributed to enhancing the security posture of the organizations he has worked for by integrating cutting-edge technologies with best practices in policy and governance.

West's contributions extend beyond the confines of his day-to-day professional endeavors. He is a prolific author and a respected voice in the cybersecurity community, contributing to leading journals, blogs, and speaking at international conferences on topics ranging from cyber threat intelligence to blockchain security. His insights and analyses are highly sought for their depth, clarity, and applicability.

In academia, West has served as a guest lecturer at several universities, where he has taught on cybersecurity, ethical hacking, and information assurance. He is passionate about educating the next generation of cybersecurity professionals and sharing his knowledge and experiences to inspire and cultivate talent.

Beyond his professional achievements, West advocates for cybersecurity awareness and education among the general public. He has led numerous initiatives to increase digital literacy and promote safe online practices, contributing to a more secure digital environment for all.

Jim West's career is characterized by a relentless pursuit of excellence, a deep commitment to the cybersecurity profession, and an unwavering dedication to protecting the digital frontier. As he continues to push the boundaries of what is possible in cybersecurity, his work remains vital in the fight against cybercrime and in ensuring the safety and security of information systems worldwide.

In his seminal paper, "Beyond the CIA Triad," West expounds upon the foundational principles of cybersecurity, transcending the traditional paradigm of Confidentiality, Integrity, and Availability (CIA) to encompass a comprehensive framework comprising nine core principles. Jim West is considered exceptional in his roles as a cybersecurity expert and an author. With more than 32 years of experience in IT and cybersecurity, West has a deep and broad understanding of the field. He has worked across diverse sectors, including commercial, space, federal, and defense, highlighting his versatile expertise.

West's disciplined commitment to continued learning spans several prestigious certifications, including penetration testing, network and system auditing, risk management, solution engineering, security architecture, and more. These certifications demonstrate his commitment to staying at the forefront of the cybersecurity profession and continuing to exceed industry standards.

Through his extensive experience in industry certifications, West developed proprietary methods for mastering knowledge quickly and effectively. In the early 2000s, while working overseas at Camp Slayer, Iraq, West first noticed the difficulty service members experienced in preparing for life after active duty. Knowing the opportunities available in cybersecurity, he began working with service members to train and obtain certifications in their downtime to prepare for cybersecurity positions and government contract work opportunities.

West has authored several books, including "Cybersecurity and Test Tips," which is still listed as one of the "100 Best Cybersecurity Books of All Time" by Bookauthority.org and, unironically, is his most illegally pirated and plagiarized work to date. Since its publication in June 2015, it has been illegally downloaded more than 500,000 times across the globe.

The in-person coaching West developed in the early 2000s served as the proving grounds for what he would later build his company TopCyberPro.com in 2020. TopCyberPro.com's mission is to bridge the cybersecurity skills gap by providing affordable training, coaching, and mentoring to individuals of all backgrounds and skill levels to help them break into an ever-expanding industry. This initiative reflects his dedication to empowering others and improving the cybersecurity workforce.

As an Author, West's "Magicae Mathematica" series uniquely blends elements of history, mathematics, and magic to create engaging and educational stories for young readers. His ability to make complex subjects like mathematics accessible and exciting for children is a testament to his creativity and teaching skills. The "Magicae Mathematica" series has been well-received, with its first book, "Libellus de Numeros," and subsequent titles praised for their innovative plots and educational value. This series entertains and encourages a love for learning among its readers. His background in cybersecurity and his role as a father influence his writing, drawing from his professional and personal experiences to create relatable and inspiring characters and scenarios, adding depth and authenticity to his stories.

By excelling in his professional career and his creative endeavors, Jim West demonstrates a unique blend of technical prowess, educational commitment, and creative talent. This combination makes him a standout figure in both fields and contributes to his reputation as one of the greatest in his areas of expertise.

Also by Jim West:

Cybersecurity Test Tips and Methods (2015)
Project Management Exam Study Guide (2015)
STFU.GOYA.GID: A Self-Start Guide (2015)
Active Learning (2017)
Time for Time Management (2018)
One Sheet Resume (2019)
Public Speaking Tips (2019)
BOOSH!: Maximize Your Productivity (2020)
NTK Dictonary for Open Book Exams (2023)
Resume Remix (2023)
CISSP in 10 Days (2023)
CISSP in 30 Days (2023)

To connect with West on LinkedIn, scan the QR code below:

For more information, visit:
https://www.JimWestAuthor.com

# WOUNDED WARRIOR PROJECT®

A portion of the proceeds of the purchase of this book will be donated to the Wounded Warrior Project.

Wounded Warrior Project (WWP) began in 2003 as a small, grassroots effort providing simple care and comfort items to the hospital bedsides of the first wounded service members returning home from the conflicts in Iraq and Afghanistan.

As their post-service needs evolved, so have their programs and services. Today, through the direct programs in mental health, career counseling, and long-term rehabilitative care, along with our advocacy efforts, WWP improves the lives of millions of warriors and their families.

Mission: To honor and empower wounded warriors.
Vision: To Foster the most successful, well-adjusted generation of wounded service members in our nation's history.

This effort requires the passion and commitment of friends, supporters, and like-minded organizations that enable us to fulfill our mission. With their collaboration and support, WWP strives to ensure that when those who serve come home, they're afforded every opportunity to be as successful as a civilian as they were in the military.

To donate to the Wounded Warrior Project, scan the QR code below:

For more information, visit:
https://www.woundedwarriorproject.org/mission